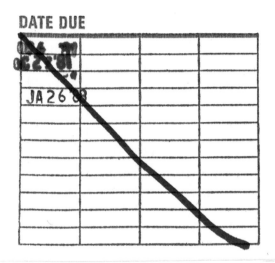

INDIAN POLICE
AND JUDGES

Experiments in
Acculturation and Control

by WILLIAM T. HAGAN

University of Nebraska Press
Lincoln and London

First Bison Book printing: 1980

Most recent printing indicated by first digit below:
1   2   3   4   5   6   7   8   9   10

Library of Congress Cataloging in Publication Data

Hagan, William Thomas.
    Indian police and judges.

    Reprint of the ed. published by Yale University Press, which was issued as no. 13 of its series: Yale Western Americana series.
    Bibliography: p. 177
    Includes index.
    1. Indians of North America—Courts.   2. Indians of North America—Justice, Administration of.   I.   Title.   II.   Series: Yale Western Americana series ; 13.
KF8225.5.H3   1980   301.24'1   79–18496
ISBN 0–8032–2308–0
ISBN 0–8032–7205–7 pbk.

Reprinted by arrangement with Yale University Press
Manufactured in the United States of America

TO

Tom, Martha, Dan, and Sarah, who perplex and delight

Preface

ON SEVERAL RESERVATIONS today may be seen Indian police
and judges, remnants of a system which once provided
law and order for tribesmen in the great reservation era of
the late nineteenth century. They have survived the dissolution of most of these reservations and the attempts to
integrate their people into the dominant society.

Since 1950 there has been much discussion of transferring
civil and criminal jurisdiction over Indians, in those states
where it has been exercised by the federal government, to
the states themselves. In 1953 Congress did this for five
states and authorized others to do so on their own initiative.
President Eisenhower signed the bill with some reluctance,
observing that it failed to provide for adequate consideration of Indian wishes in the matter.

This policy has become highly controversial. Developing
concurrently with a political awareness by American Indians, it has produced a debate featuring charges that local
law enforcement agents are discriminating against Indians.
The quotation attributed in 1962 to a police chief in a town
on the old Pine Ridge Reservation in South Dakota illustrates one facet of the problem: "The Indian is not a law-
abiding person. As near as I can figure out, it's about like
the Negroes down South: You can't let them get the upper
hand."[1]

A congressional committee and the Federal Civil Rights
Commission have investigated the specific charges and the
general problem of providing law for American Indians.

1. *New York Times* (June 13, 1962), p. 41.

Their reports reveal a point of view similar to the attitude
that resulted in trying the first Indian police and judges.
Despite the passage of three quarters of a century, law and
law enforcement for our citizens of Indian extraction still
constitute a complex problem. And as Dean Acheson noted
in his dissent to the report of the First Hoover Commission,
which initiated the policy of federal withdrawal from Indian
affairs, memories of the experiences of the Cherokees with
the state of Georgia "make a novice in this field pause before
endorsing a recommendation to assimilate the Indian, and
turn him, his culture, and his means of livelihood over to
state control."

In the preparation of this study I have been aided by
grants from the Faculty Research Fund of North Texas
State University and by numerous individuals, particularly
the staffs of the North Texas State University Library, the
Oklahoma Historical Society, the National Archives, the
Federal Record Centers in Denver and Fort Worth, the
Denver Public Library, the Smithsonian Institution, and the
State Historical Society of Colorado.

My former colleague Chester A. Newland read most of
the manuscript and made helpful suggestions on points of
law and public administration. Another former colleague,
W. Keith Eubank, interrupted his own work many times to
help me resolve nagging questions of style. To the members
of my immediate family I owe a special debt of gratitude for
typing and proofreading services. And some of the most
pleasant memories associated with this project are those of
the afternoon my wife and I heard Mrs. Samuel R. Sixkiller
of Muskogee, Oklahoma, reminisce about her husband and
their years with the Indian Service.

                                                        W.T.H.

Fredonia, New York
1965

Contents

List of Illustrations

Following page 194

Abbreviations in Footnotes

AR	Annual Report
LB	Letter Book
CIA	Commissioner of Indian Affairs
OIALB	Office of Indian Affairs, Letter Book
OIALR	Office of Indian Affairs, Letters Received
ser.	Government Document Serial Set

1. The Subjects of the Experiments

In 1956 in an adultery case involving the Sioux Indians Marie Little Finger and David Black Cat, a United States circuit judge upheld the jurisdiction of a tribal court, citing the existence of such tribunals since 1883. The Indian courts and the police forces from which their judges were originally drawn stemmed from the conditions on Indian reservations after the Civil War. It was a troubled period in the West as the last of the Indian Wars were fought. Crazy Horse, Sitting Bull, and Gall led the Sioux and Cheyenne hordes against the 7th Cavalry on the Little Big Horn, Joseph of the Nez Percé shepherded his people toward the Canadian border while fighting off three American columns, and Cochise and Geronimo of the Chiricahua Apaches terrorized the Southwest. Although Sitting Bull escaped to Canada, and Geronimo did not surrender until 1886, most of the former hostiles were dead or settled on reservations by 1878.

The same era saw almost as much confusion in the Bureau of Indian Affairs and in the special congressional committees as on the reservations. Revelations of graft and corruption in the administration of reservations were matched by conflicting policies in Washington and a natural revulsion against the seemingly endless bloodletting on the plains. It all led to a re-examination of our basic approach to the Indian problem. The first effort was by a congressional committee, appointed in 1865, which traveled extensively, gathering testimony from members of the Indian service, army personnel, frontiersmen, and Indians; its doleful conclusion was that the Indian was on the road to extinction. Although the committee called only for patching up the current system, its recommendations did lead to the creation of a new commission in 1867 with instructions to try to eliminate some of the causes of plains warfare.

With army representation headed by William Tecumseh Sherman, joined by the Commissioner of Indian Affairs, the chairman of the Senate Committee on Indian Affairs, and Samuel F. Tappan from the ranks of the reformers, the commission negotiated treaties and framed a report. The treaties were designed to further concentrate the Plains Indian population and thus reduce the friction between it and the white settlers. The report called for the extension of government over the Indians and the introduction of missionaries and teachers to assist in their civilization. These did not represent revolutionary concepts, since the hope of converting the nomad pagan warrior into a peaceful Christian farmer was of long standing.

The most sweeping change being discussed was the proposed transfer of the Bureau of Indian Affairs from the Interior Department back to the War Department, from which it had been detached in 1849. The army spokesmen vigorously advocated this, as did some members of Congress. They maintained that only the bayonet would persuade the red man to leave his war pony for the plow. Indian Service personnel and the reformers were vehemently opposed to the Bureau's return to the War Department, arguing that only peaceful persuasion could truly civilize. The debate continued into the 1890s and soured relations between civilians and the military at a time when their utmost cooperation was demanded by the problems on the plains. Probably the military would have carried the day had it not been for the volume of protests from the reformers. And the concept of Indian police forces did give the opponents of the military an alternative to reliance on troops. It is in this perspective that the police policy became so important in the interdepartmental squabbling.

The reformers, generally Easterners or transplanted Easterners like Bishop Henry Benjamin Whipple who had moved to Minnesota from New York, multiplied their influence in the 1880s when they merged their efforts in organizations like the Indian Rights Association and the Indian Citizenship Committee of Boston. With one exception, Dr. T. A. Bland's National Indian Defense Association, they agreed on the necessity of speeding acculturation of the red men. Through their well-publicized informal conferences at Lake Mohonk, the aid of friendly members of Congress like Senator Dawes, and the editorial support of leading eastern newspapers, they maintained a steady pressure on the government and helped thwart the plans of the military to recapture the conduct of Indian affairs. In general, the reformers approved the innovations in Indian policy during the administration of the Presidents from Grant to McKinley. Their complaint was that not enough changes were being made.

Prominent in the ranks of the reformers were members of the Society of Friends, as active here as they had been in other humanitarian movements from the early eighteenth century. To them must be given credit for the first substantial experiment in improving Indian administration—Grant's Quaker or Peace Policy. It involved two principal innovations: seeking recommendations from church groups for appointments to the Indian Service, and the creation of a Board of Indian Commissioners to advise the government on Indian matters. The quality of the Indian agents did improve, although it was soon apparent that not even the

church was always able to discern in nominees the char-
acteristics essential to honest and humane Indian administration. Unfortunately, squabbles among the religious leaders, particularly between Protestants and Roman Catholics
over the allotment of agencies, were in some respects more
demoralizing than the differences between the bureaucrats
and the army officers, because such conduct was not expected
from men of the cloth. Nor did the Board of Indian Commissioners prove as salutary in its impact as had been hoped.
The ten men who served without pay did bring about a
substantial improvement in the purchase and distribution of
goods for the Indian. Their advice on real changes in Indian
policy, however, was seldom followed. By 1900 the Board
of Indian Commissioners still met, debated, and proposed,
but had little real effect in shaping policy. It would finally
be dissolved during the period of the Indian New Deal,
when Secretary of the Interior Harold Ickes and Commissioner of Indian Affairs John Collier collaborated in developing new policies in Indian affairs.

The plans for civilizing the Indian, plans which had general support among both the bureaucrats in Washington and
the reformers, assumed the necessity of providing law for
the Indian. In the East the principal benefit envisioned was
the protection of property rights, which were supposed to
lure the Indian down the white man's road. He would thus
come to appreciate the difference between *meum* and *tuum,*
his failure to do so having disturbed observers from Peter
Martyr to Henry L. Dawes. The Dawes Act of 1887 was
simply the application on a large scale of the principle of
ownership of land in severalty, which already was generally
accepted and had been implemented previously on a small
scale. The law provided machinery for allotting the land
of specified tribes. Each member of such a tribe would
receive a plot of land, and the surplus, after this division,

would then be sold to whites, thus "opening" the reservation. But what was to be gained by destroying the concept of communal ownership, if the new property owner had no legal machinery to protect his rights?

In the West the extension of law over the Indian was seen as more of an answer to administrative problems. Supervising an Indian reservation in this era was no sinecure. In particular, reservations housing recent hostiles were nerve-racking assignments. Despite close surveillance the tribesmen managed to retain some weapons, and previous outbreaks had demonstrated how far a handful of determined Indians could go with a few rusty revolvers and battered rifles. Recalcitrant chiefs were backed by hot-blooded warriors, and liquor smuggled into Indian camps aggravated the situation. A Cheyenne agent once reported seeing 1,200 of his charges "drunk as loons."[1] Horse thieves among the renegade whites did their bit by running off Indian ponies and keeping young warriors restive. Such action, as one official predicted, could evoke Indian retaliation: "Then our senators asked Congress to furnish the Governor with arms to aid the border settlers and defend themselves against the Indian raiders."[2] In such fashion were Indian wars born. Little wonder that harassed agents, miles from the nearest army post and unable to communicate with their sullen charges except through interpreters, slept fitfully.

Army personnel were equally nervous and sometimes trigger-happy, as was indicated by the number of Indians killed resisting arrest or while in custody. In extenuation the soldiers could cite the case of Crazy Horse who, ordered imprisoned on suspicion of planning an outbreak, drew a

1. Donald J. Berthrong, *The Southern Cheyennes* (Norman, 1963), p. 374.
2. Ibid., p. 383.

knife and died fighting to avoid being locked up. Or they might evoke the example of the old Kiowa war chief Satank, who, singing his death song, took the same course rather than submit to transportation to Texas for trial on murder charges.

On older reservations such as those in eastern Oklahoma the whites did not fear for their scalps, but they had problems enough. Agents, frequently political hacks with no previous experience with Indians, tried to administer areas the size of Connecticut, populated by tribesmen some of whom still held tenaciously to their native ways. The agency staffs, small and possibly qualified by nothing more than being related to the agent or a politician, were of limited assistance. Simply procuring information on conditions in the far corners of the reservation became a difficult task when a rider on an Indian pony represented the fastest means of communication.

As the local representative of the United States government and the fount of all favors, the agent found much of his time consumed in arbitrating local issues. A single day might see him called upon to locate a fence line, determine ownership of a maverick calf, and reconcile a glowering husband and irate wife. An Osage agent lamented that "every conceivable complaint that can arise in a frontier country for settlement, and for which there is no law or regulation" was turned over to him for adjudication.[3] And enforcement of his decisions in the absence of police or military force obviously posed problems.

Although their presence frequently was necessary to intimidate potential hostiles, or simply to reassure a timid administrator, soldiers complicated an agent's problems. Indian women near troop bivouacs were drawn into pros-

3. Annual Report (AR) of Wm. J. Pollock, 1899 in *Annual Reports of the Secretary of the Interior* (ser. 3915, p. 296).

titution or casual alliances, and Indians of both sexes were debauched by alcohol. As one administrator observed bitingly, there was an "inevitable demoralization of intemperance and lewdness which comes to a reservation from a camp of soldiers."[4]

Another constant source of trouble for agents was the contact of their charges with certain types of white civilians. Some of the human debris which the moving frontier had deposited on Indian land became squaw men by marriage into the tribe and proceeded to dabble in reservation politics, contributing to the already rampant factionalism. Many lived by peddling liquor to the Indians or by other means calculated to contribute to reservation unrest. Judge Isaac Charles Parker, of Indian Territory fame, referred to them as the "froth of the billows" on the "tide of emigration." These "refugees from justice" were charged by the judge with introducing the Indians to "every form of demoralization and disease with which depraved humanity in its most degrading forms is ever afflicted."[5] Judge Parker was an authority on these topics; in his two decades on the bench he sent eighty-eight assorted white, Indian, and mixed-blood outlaws through the trap of the Fort Smith gallows.

In the 1870s life was as cheap in the eastern Oklahoma home of the Five Civilized Tribes as anywhere in the United States. A contemporary saying: "There is no Sunday west of St. Louis—no God west of Fort Smith," summed up the situation succinctly.[6] The absence of a territorial or state government left law enforcement in the hands of the officials of the ineffective tribal governments and the deputies of

4. AR of Edward P. Smith, 1875 (ser. 1680, p. 521).

5. Fred Harvey Harrington, *Hanging Judge* (Caldwell, 1951), p. 165.

6. Glenn Shirley, *Law West of Fort Smith* (New York, 1961), p. 83.

Judge Parker's court, who proved incapable of containing a
population including renegade whites, Negro outlaws, and
Indians of every conceivable blood mixture and degree of
civilization. When the likes of Bob Dalton, Belle Starr,
Smokey Mankiller, and Blue Duck were sober, they were
dangerous; when they imbibed Choctaw beer (a potent brew
of hops, barley, fishberries, and tobacco), they were also
unpredictable.

Judge Parker took the bench at Fort Smith in 1875 and
in his first term of court signaled a new era by sentencing
eight men to be hanged. The slaying of sixty-five of his
deputies in the next twenty years indicates both the persistence of his efforts and his lack of success in introducing
order.[7] When Judge Parker died in 1896, Indian Territory
was still an exciting place to live.

Judge Parker's deputies were no answer to the problem
of law enforcement on the average Indian reservation. Nor
was the agent's own staff sufficiently large or well trained
to undertake these supplementary duties. On a typical reservation the staff might number less than a dozen, including
laborers, clerks, a blacksmith, a teacher or two for the agency
schools, and a couple of "farmers" assigned to instruct
apathetic ex-warriors in the use of hoes and plows.

The farmers and the teachers, the latter possibly sponsored
by some religious denomination and doubling as missionaries, represented three of the standard approaches to civilizing the Indian now that he had been pacified. The standard
formula was, to educate him, Christianize him, and convert
him from hunting to farming. But there was a growing
feeling that the formula lacked something. As the model
Indian began to adapt to civilized ways by tilling a plot of
ground and wearing "citizen's dress"—nineteenth-century

7. Homer Croy, *He Hanged Them High* (New York, 1952), p. 6.

jargon for shirt and trousers in place of blanket and leggings
—he would begin to accumulate property. But property in
Indian society had no protection comparable to that in
white society.[8] Two Episcopal churchmen, both vocal friends
of the Indian, saw the need clearly. Bishop Henry Benjamin
Whipple had advised President Lincoln: "They cannot live
without law. We have broken up, in part, their tribal relations, and they must have something in their place."[9] His
fellow bishop, William Hobart Hare, warned: "The efforts
of civil agents, teachers, and missionaries are like the strug-
gles of drowning men weighted with lead as long as, by
absence of law, Indian society is left without a base."[10]
Beginning in the 1820s and continuing into the 1870s, a
succession of Secretaries of War and of the Interior, together
with Commissioners of Indian Affairs, had voiced sentiments
comparable to those of the bishops. Moreover, on those
reservations where the chiefs were aligned with Conservative
factions—those most attached to their native culture—there
were obvious advantages to supplanting the chiefs with a
force more appreciative of the virtues of civilization and
amenable to the agent's will.

Indian police and Indian judges looking to the agent for

8. As the very first Commissioner of Indian Affairs Elbert Herring
observed in 1832: "the absence of *meum* and *tuum* in the general community of possessions, which is the grand conservative principle of the
social state, is a perpetual cause of the *vis inertiae* of savage life." AR of
Herring, 1832 (ser. 233, p. 163). For the same sentiment twenty years
later, see a communication by Indian Agent A. M. Coffee: "Until the
rights of property, the distinctions of *meum* and *tuum,* are recognised;
until the wrongdoer himself can be made to feel the punishment due to
his misdeeds, it will be vain to expect that reform, morally or physically,
so much desired by our government." AR of Coffee, 1851 (ser. 611,
p. 353).

9. Henry Benjamin Whipple, *Lights and Shadows of a Long Episcopate* (New York, 1902), p. 512.

10. William Justin Harsha, "Law For the Indians," *North American
Review* (March 1882), p. 284.

direction might answer many of the problems confronting that harassed official. In the last quarter of the nineteenth century they were appointed among most of the Indians in the American West excepting, principally, the Pueblos. The police and judges represented an infusion of Anglo-Saxon legal concepts but, to be really effective in more than preserving order, they had to build on native institutions.

Whites had first erred in overestimating the strength of Indian political institutions, and then had gone to the other extreme and ignored the stability they did provide. As early as 1831, John Marshall in *Cherokee Nation v. Georgia* had rejected the theory that Indian tribes were the equivalent of independent foreign nations. Nevertheless, until 1871 and the replacement by Congress of treaties with agreements to be ratified by both Houses, this fiction had been maintained. It was a rare Indian tribe that had the cohesiveness the tribal designation implied. On the plains the standard unit was the band, a tribe being composed of several bands, the number and membership of which were in continual flux. Each had its own leaders, wandered as it chose, and would be physically united with all the other bands of the tribe for only a few weeks of the year. Even in the eastern woodlands, "tribe" implied more than was usually the case for the seminomadic Indians of that area. What the Americans referred to as a tribe probably would consist of several villages scattered over a considerable area, each going its own way, even in matters of war and peace.[11] Simply herding all the members of the different villages, or different bands, onto one reservation and singling out a prominent and amenable Indian as the principal chief, produced no real tribal unity. In short, it would appear that the loss of tribal

11. For example, most of the Sacs and Foxes were not hostile in the Black Hawk War, nor were most of the Seminoles at any given moment in their war.

cohesiveness noted by the reformers and administrators probably had never existed in the sense they conceived of it.

Though it appeared to the casual white observer that anarchy reigned in Indian encampments, those societies had evolved their own patterns of law and order.[12] Law in the sense of formal written codes, of course, they did not have, but there were clearly defined customary codes of behavior enforced by public opinion and religious sanctions. In the intimate life led by the typical Indian, the approval of one's immediate family and clan members was of the highest importance. For most Indians the prospect of scornful glances and derisive laughter from the circle around the campfire was the chief instrument of social control. All the social and political ties of the Indians, moreover, had strong religious overtones so that the supernatural played a larger role in maintaining peace and order in their communities than in contemporary American society. As in the Massachusetts Bay Colony, there was a close correlation in Indian communities between sin and crime. Separation of church and state was not an Indian concept.

Among those Plains tribes which had only recently been forced onto the reservations, some of the most spectacular experiments with Indian police and judges took place. And, happily, anthropologists have studied the legal institutions

12. The following discussion is based principally upon Henry Ellin, "The Northern Arapaho of Wyoming," and John H. Provinse, "The Underlying Sanctions of Plains Indian Culture," both in Fred Eggan, ed., *Social Anthropology of North American Tribes* (Chicago, 1955); George Bird Grinnell, *The Fighting Cheyennes* (Norman, 1956); K. N. Llewellyn and E. Adamson Hoebel, *The Cheyenne Way* (Norman, 1941); Robert H. Lowie, "Property Rights and Coercive Powers of Plains Indian Military Societies," in *Journal of Legal and Political Sociology* (April 1943); Symmes C. Oliver, *Ecology and Cultural Continuity As Continuing Factors in the Social Organization of the Plains Indians* (Berkeley, 1962); Jane Richardson, *Law and Status Among the Kiowa Indians* (New York, 1940).

of the Plains tribes more closely than those of any other
Indians. Their studies reveal some points of similarity and
many points of difference among native law-ways of these
people, diversity being the rule here as in any aspect of
Indian cultures. Standards of right and wrong varied widely
from tribe to tribe, as did the procedures for punishing
transgressors.

In all Plains tribes, since they accorded highest status to
those who demonstrated bravery and daring in battle, individual aggressive drives were vented against outsiders. The
result is a pattern of crime unlike anything in white society.
Offenses against property were insignificant because Indian
society stressed cooperation and sharing. Hunger drove no
one to steal where sharing was a cardinal virtue. And the
very scarcity of personal possessions would make a stolen
article too conspicuous to be used in a tightly knit society
where everyone was constantly on view. Therefore theft was
virtually unknown, although some Indians had bad reputa-
tions for borrowing without first seeking the owner's permission. If the borrowed item were a horse, in a society which
placed great value on horses for hunting and fighting and
as symbols of affluence, the "borrowing" could lead to
trouble.

Among crimes they regarded as serious, homicide, adultery, and violations of communal hunt rules appear to have
been the most prevalent among the Plains tribes. Here also,
the usual variations appeared. Among the Cheyennes violations of the sex code seem to have been infrequent, whereas
among the Kiowas they were among the most frequent
sources of trouble. Homicide did not occur so often as one
might expect in a society that glorified the warrior, because
intertribal warfare served as an outlet for aggressive drives.
Violations of communal hunt rules much more frequently
led to dissension. It was a very serious offense when one

thoughtless individual frightened away game, causing the entire tribe to enter the winter short of meat, hides for new tipis, and robes to protect them from the fierce northers.

Punishment of such a transgressor was more of an individual responsibility than in white society. For perhaps ten or eleven months of the year the tribe was separated into bands and wandered across the plains as the meandering of the buffalo dictated, or holed up in some sheltered valley in the depths of winter. Each band moved under its own chief or chiefs and punished its own criminals. An Indian abducting another man's wife or stealing his favorite horse might be dealt with by the victim personally. If the offender were a tribesman of no particular consequence, and the offended a headman, the punishment would likely be immediate and severe. If the status situation were reversed, the offender might escape unscathed, although publicity could damage his position in the community. If the incident featured two prominent and influential members, the other headmen might arbitrate to prevent a serious disruption of band unity.

The best-known device among the Plains Indians for maintaining harmony and punishing transgressors was the military or soldiers' society. It functioned, however, for only a few weeks in the summer when the clans united for the Sun Dance religious ceremonies and an annual buffalo hunt. The exceptions to it were the Comanches, who had no military societies, and the Cheyennes and the Teton Sioux, whose societies functioned the year round.

Membership in the societies, of which each tribe usually had several, was open to all able-bodied males—the tribe's warriors. Operating under a variety of names—the Dog Soldiers and the Kit Foxes of the Cheyennes, and the Tomahawks of the Arapahoes, to name only three—they were not a law unto themselves but, rather, carried out the will of the tribe as expressed through the chiefs or tribal councils.

Their heaviest responsibilities were in those areas of activity most vital to the tribe as a whole. When the tribe moved as a unit, they policed the line of march, scouting ahead, covering the flanks, and keeping the column closed up by prodding the stragglers. When the tribe reached its camping ground, they determined the location of the lodges in the customary circle and maintained order throughout the camp. During buffalo-hunting season the members of the society selected to act as police enforced the rules which forbade early killing at the expense of the entire group of hunters.

Violators of the tribal codes were subject to varying punishments, even those guilty of committing the identical crime. The penalties ranged from ridicule to banishment or execution. Imprisonment was unknown; fines, in the form of compensation for the offended, were the most common punishment imposed. Even murder might be compromised in this way if the slayer were a man of prominence and the slain of little consequence. The same principle was applied on a larger scale when the tribe assumed responsibility and sought to pacify white authorities or another tribe. A gift of horses might redress the wrong, or weapons or blankets might be used "to cover the dead." Land cessions were employed on occasion to appease the United States for crimes against whites. And it became official United States policy to exact compensation for damages to whites or their property by withholding annuities due the guilty individuals or tribes. In cases involving Indians only, there was no flat rate as in the Anglo-Saxon *wergeld*. Among the Plains Indians, as with the Yurok tribe of California, the compensation varied with the status of those involved. The tears of the widow of a Comanche or Cheyenne of little import might be dried by the payment of two or three horses and a rifle; to assuage the grief for the death of a prominent warrior would require a more substantial property settlement.

An incident involving another non-Plains tribe, the Navajo, illustrates how difficult it was for Indians and whites to appreciate the law-ways of the other. Sixty Indian horses had been killed for cropping grass on a pasture reserved for the mounts of a fort's garrison. Unable to secure compensation for their horses, a Navajo sought satisfaction by killing a Negro slave of the post's commanding officer. When the white man did not see the justice in this destruction of his property, the Indians tried to mollify him by killing a Mexican slave from the Indian camp and depositing the evidence of their sacrifice in the fort. Once again there was a complete lack of comprehension of each other's motives, resulting in an often encountered reaction—a punitive expedition was sent out from the fort against the "hostiles."[13]

Such property destruction as the killing of the Negro slave was a common form of punishment. If the offense was jumping a buffalo herd before the signal was given, the tribal soldiers might mete out justice on the spot by smashing the culprit's rifle or shooting his horse. Man-Lying-on-His-Back-with-His-Legs-Flexed once inadvertently violated hunt rules, and the Cheyenne soldiers destroyed his lodge.[14] On another occasion the soldiers might have contented themselves with penalizing the impulsive one by delaying his start until the other hunters had given chase or, if the infraction were particularly flagrant, they might have whipped the offender with horse quirts. Cuckolded husbands took such direct action or worse. In rare cases the victim, his kin, or members of the police would kill the offender or drive him from camp. Banishment, perhaps for years, was a punishment the Cheyennes reserved for murder of the inexcusable variety

13. Ruth M. Underhill, *The Navajos* (Norman, 1956), pp. 106–07. For the army version of this incident, see L. R. Bailey, *The Long Walk* (Los Angeles, 1964), pp. 84–89.

14. Llewellyn and Hoebel, *The Cheyenne Way*, pp. 116–17.

which they regarded as both a crime and a sin; they believed the killer's viscera would rot, emitting a putrid odor which would frighten away the buffalo upon which the tribe depended. The murderer's action also bloodied the sacred feathers, and these religious objects required purification ceremonies before the Cheyennes would be restored to supernatural favor. Even if readmitted to the tribal circle, the murderer was regarded as contaminating anything he used, and he suffered a form of ostracism, others refusing to smoke, drink, or eat with him. There were even rare instances of a deceased murderer's children suffering social discrimination long after his death.

The strength of public opinion as a restraining force was most apparent in the use of ridicule as punishment. The ears or tail of an offender's horse might be cropped or, as in the case of the Cheyenne warrior Big-Footed Bull, who violated hunt rules, his blanket was torn into strips to be worn by the soldiers during the tribal dances, thus advertising his disgrace.[15] Unfaithful wives had the tips of their noses sliced off by jealous husbands, and bore for the rest of their lives conspicuous marks of their infidelity. Just having some unpopular act singled out for loud, disparaging comment among the lodges held the individual up to ridicule and had a chastening effect in such closely knit societies. For prematurely discharging his rifle and aborting an attempt to run off the mounts of cavalry troopers trailing his people during their famed flight, the Nez Percé warrior Otskai's punishment was to be scorned by his fellow tribesmen. A white man reporting the incident, and unappreciative of the weight of ridicule in Indian society, cited Otskai's punishment as evidence of lack of military discipline among the Nez Percés.[16]

15. Ibid., p. 113.
16. Francis Haines, *The Nez Percés* (Norman, 1955), p. 260.

The Kiowas inflicted such embarrassment and ridicule on a criminal that he reportedly soon died. The man was a chronic rapist who was finally taught the error of his ways by the women: they laid an ambush and baited the trap with a beautiful young girl. When he took the bait, they suddenly appeared and overpowered him. As others held him helpless on the ground, each women in turn raised her skirts and sat on his face. The experience was not itself fatal, but the loss of status stemming from the derision it inspired was.[17] The possibility of such drastic punishment was perhaps more chastening in its effect than the threat of the electric chair in more sophisticated societies.

As in medieval Europe, there were Plains societies which provided a type of sanctuary for infringers of the tribe's codes. Among the Kiowas it took the form of refuge in a tipi housing the medicine bundle, the collection of objects sacred to the clan. Since violence in the presence of the bundle might bring down the wrath of the gods on the entire tribe, miscreants could escape the police by taking sanctuary near the bundle. Keepers of the bundle also acted as intermediaries and helped bring the offender and offended together to smoke a peace pipe. If the offender offered what appeared to be fair compensation for the wrong he had done, his victim, having smoked the pipe, must accept the settlement. Not to do so would incur unfavorable comment and bad luck because he had flouted the supernatural powers of the peace pipe.

Counterparts of these practices might have been found in an earlier era among the neighbors of the Plains tribes. For example, the Omahas, the Sacs and Foxes, and the Winnebagoes had had men's societies which played comparable police roles. But these tribes had been submerged

17. Richardson, *Law and Status Among the Kiowa Indians,* p. 35.

earlier by the white tidal wave and, when officials of the
Office of Indian Affairs were considering the problem of
law enforcement on reservations in the 1870s, their political
structure had been so altered that little remained of those
institutions. Indeed, tribes like the Winnebagoes and the
Sacs and Foxes had been so battered and degraded that they
had lost most of their capacity for self-government. Although the police power of the men's societies of these tribes
might be only a faint memory, as late as 1890 a Cheyenne
and Arapaho agent would complain that on his reservation
the Dog Soldiers, as he called them, were strengthening the
hand of reactionary chiefs.[18]

If in the 1870s the Plains Indians and their devotion to
their native ways represented one end of the spectrum, and
tribes like the Winnebagoes, and Sacs and Foxes, symbolized
the slough of despond in the middle, the Indians known
as the Five Civilized Tribes after their removal to Oklahoma
represented the other extreme. After two centuries of contact with the whites they had evolved an approach to the
maintenance of law and order which strongly resembled
institutions among the whites. Led by their educated full-
bloods and mixed-bloods, particularly the latter, they wrote
constitutions and codes of laws, built jails, appointed sheriffs,
and formed their equivalent of a police force, the Lighthorse.

In their aboriginal state in the Southeast the Five Civilized
Tribes (Cherokees, Creeks, Seminoles, Choctaws, and
Chickasaws) had exhibited the same cultural diversity to be
expected among any five tribes inhabiting a given region.
As with the Plains societies, these Indians relied chiefly on
the pressure of public opinion to maintain peace and order.
Violators of tribal law-ways were usually punished by the
injured party or by his friends and relations. Again, as with

18. AR of Charles F. Ashley, 1890 (ser. 2841, p. 177).

the Plains Indians, the cohesiveness and intimacy of tribal society resulted in a relatively low crime rate.

In contact with white men from the seventeenth century, the Five Civilized Tribes had made considerable progress toward acculturation. By the time the Office of Indian Affairs sought to recruit Indian police forces, these tribes had a familiarity with American legal institutions greater than that of any other Indians involved in the police experiment. The Cherokees provide an excellent case study of adaptation to the legal institutions of their white neighbors and conquerors. Indicative of the difficult transition they were undergoing, they seemed to provide more than their share of both outlaws and industrious farmers, of both advanced political institutions and bloody feuds.

In their native state, perhaps the most striking feature of the law-ways of Cherokees and other southern Indians was their use of sanctuaries. Cherokee miscreants were usually safe if they could make it to one of the towns hallowed by tradition as a refuge. Otherwise their machinery for maintaining law and order resembled that of other tribes we have noted, except for the absence of soldier societies.

By 1800 the Cherokees were already showing progress in civilization. Looms, plows, and wagons were used widely among the tribesmen, and a few progressive mixed-bloods were farming on a scale that placed them in the planter category, complete with slaves. The relatively rapid rate of acculturation of these Indians is to be explained by the dedicated teaching of missionaries and the interest of white fathers in their mixed-blood offspring. More whites intermarried with the Cherokees than with any of the other Five Civilized Tribes.[19]

19. Grant Foreman, *The Five Civilized Tribes* (Norman, 1934), p. 360.

As the leading Cherokees accumulated property, they became interested in adopting legal practices of the whites to safeguard their newfound wealth. The first printed law of which we have record dates from 1808 and provides a penalty of a hundred lashes for horse theft. The other laws to be passed in this last century of the Cherokees' self-government reflected their concern for property. For example, all the cases coming before the Cherokee High Court during its first term involved property. This is understandable in view of the dominant role played in Cherokee government by the propertied minority. Indeed, sensitiveness about slave property produced laws among the Five Civilized Tribes as reactionary as any enacted by white governments in the deep South.

As the Cherokees developed a legal code, they provided machinery for enforcement. A full decade before their first laws were written, they had appointed warriors to assist the chiefs in dealing with horse thieves. The same council that in 1808 wrote the law on horse theft formalized the procedure by creating "regulating" companies consisting of two officers and four privates, to be paid from annuities received from the United States. Popularly known as "Lighthorse" and imitated by the other Civilized Tribes, they performed the function of police. Criminals apprehended by them were turned over to the tribal courts for trial and punishment.

The Cherokees tried several court systems, and their laws appear harsh and barbaric by modern standards. Rapists for the first offense were "punished with fifty lashes upon the bare back and the left ear cropped off close to the head; for the second offense, one hundred lashes and the other ear cut off; for the third offense, death."[20] However, when it is

20. Thomas Lee Ballenger, "The Development of Law and Legal Institutions Among the Cherokees," Ph.D. Thesis (1938), p. 36.

recollected that as late as 1829 inmates of a Massachusetts prison had the name of the institution tattooed on them, Cherokee ear cropping and use of the lash in the early nineteenth century do not appear so extreme. Indicative of the progress they hoped to make was a Cherokee law of 1810 intended as "an act of oblivion for all lives" for which the various clans and tribes "may have been indebted."[21] Clan revenge and bloody feuds, nevertheless, continued to complicate Cherokee society for many years. In 1872 the official explanation for an outburst of violence at Coody's Bluff, featuring gunfire in a polling place and the invasion of homes, stressed "the existence of organized cliques and parties, said to be pledged to defend each member when arraigned for the violation of law."[22] Perjury, loaded juries, and intimidated witnesses were incidental evidence of a debased justice.

For a period of about twenty years before the Civil War no Lighthorse operated among the Cherokees; sheriffs and their deputies exercised the police power. Revived after the war, the Lighthorse operated until the dissolution of the Cherokee government. Although on paper, Cherokee political institutions were quite sophisticated and differentiated, in practice the available Lighthorse frequently had to serve as policemen, judges, and jurors. Their job was eased in 1874 by the construction of a substantial prison at Tahlequah, presided over by a High Sheriff.

But more than a stout prison and a handful of Lighthorse were necessary to maintain law and order in eastern Oklahoma in the 1870s. Thirsty Indians and the Trade and Intercourse Act of 1834, which banned introduction of intoxicating liquors into the Indian country, created a tremendous

21. Ibid., p. 35.
22. AR of John B. Jones, 1873 (ser. 1601, p. 574).

bootlegging problem.[23] Occasionally a jug was smashed or a barrel stove in, but profits as high as $4 a gallon on bootleg liquor kept the flow constant.[24] Moreover, some complained that Cherokee Lighthorse and courts were not very conscientious in running down and punishing liquor-law violators. Where enforcement was attempted, jurisdictional squabbles between Indian and United States' courts diluted its effectiveness. In the 1870s treaties existed which granted Cherokee courts jurisdiction over all tribal members, including adopted whites. But cases of murder, robbery, assault and battery with intent to kill, and simple assault, unless the parties involved were all Indian, fell within the jurisdiction of the district court sitting at Van Buren to 1871 and after that at Fort Smith.

Even before the Civil War the Cherokees had resented the activities of federal marshals in their nation. These law officers arrested Cherokees and hauled them off to courts as much as a hundred miles distant from their fellow tribesmen. Occasionally the Indian was unable to speak enough English to understand the court procedures or summon witnesses to testify in his defense. Sometimes Cherokee courts held that they should have cognizance of the case, and they disputed the authority of overzealous marshals. One such disagreement in 1872 led to the death of eleven men in a violent gun battle in a Cherokee courtroom.

The difficulty originated in a charge of murder filed

23. The act defined Indian Country and excluded from it unauthorized persons, continued the licensing system for trade, provided for indemnification for property losses suffered by whites or Indians, and placed responsibility for maintaining law and order in the Indian Country on the Indian Department. For a full discussion of the act, see Francis Paul Prucha, *American Indian Policy In the Formative Years* (Cambridge, 1962), pp. 261–69.

24. Morris L. Wardell, *A Political History of the Cherokee Nation* (Norman, 1938), p. 264.

against Ezekiel Proctor by a Cherokee court and a charge of assault with intent to kill filed against the same man by the Fort Smith authorities. Proctor was actually undergoing trial in the Going Snake court of Judge B. H. Sixkiller, one of eight Cherokee district court judges, when a posse led by two marshals from Fort Smith attempted to seize the prisoner. Included in the posse were Cherokees of a faction bitterly hostile to Proctor and intent on either capturing or killing him, so what resulted was in a large part a by-product of Cherokee feuding. When the court refused to release Proctor to the posse, a heated exchange led to gunplay in which the prisoner desperately defended himself with a pistol snatched from a bystander. Eight of his attackers were killed and three wounded. Of Proctor's supporters three were killed and his attorney and Judge Sixkiller were hit. Although wounded in the violent exchange, Proctor managed to escape. Both he and the judge found it convenient to go into hiding.[25]

Such jurisdictional conflicts did not facilitate handling the problem of white intruders on Indian land. Theoretically, only whites married into or adopted by the tribe, or specifically licensed to work in the nation, could be present in Cherokee territory. In practice, however, whites, frequently of the most undesirable type, infiltrated in increasing numbers. Cherokee agents were sometimes able to obtain the help of federal troops in evicting the trespassers, but it was an endless task. For every intruder expelled, two seemed to take his place.

Agents pleading for the help of troops recognized that they might be trading one evil for another; one agent sought a happy medium in just enough troops to do the job, with

25. AR of John B. Jones, 1872 (ser. 1560, p. 619); Grant Foreman, "The Tragedy of Going Snake Courthouse," *Daily Oklahoman* (Oct. 7, 1934), Section C, p. 14.

a full complement of officers to keep the troops from debauching the Indians. Vincent Colyer, secretary of the Board
of Indian Commissioners, conducted a special investigation
of Indian Territory in 1869 and had personal experience of
the agents' dilemma. While in Fort Gibson his rest on several
nights was disturbed by carousing soldiers. One Sunday
morning he saw four drunken enlisted men, armed with revolvers and clubs, invade a church and scatter the wor-
shipers. Colyer intervened and the "reeling, shouting and
swearing" soldiers were about to attack the Eastern reformer
when one of them recalled having seen his commanding
officer with Colyer, and they subsided.[26]

A representative of the reformers who had adopted the
cause of the Indians, Colyer had had a salutary lesson in the
lawlessness of the Indian Territory. By the time he had
visited the Navajos, he had concluded that there was a
solution:

> As I have said before of the Cheyennes, they [the
> Navajos] need police more than military guardianship;
> give them a good, simple, and practicable code of laws,
> and a police force of equal or one-half the number of
> soldiers they now have, and you will not have any
> trouble with them.[27]

Colyer now was thinking along the same lines as the administrators in their Washington offices who were speculating on the advantages of an Indian police, and as the
agents in the field who had progressed beyond the speculating stage.

26. Report of the Hon. Vincent Colyer, 1869 (ser. 1414, pp. 519–
20).
27. Ibid., p. 532.

2. Origin of the Police

WITHOUT PROMPTING from Washington, several agents in the 1860s and 1870s concluded that conditions on their reservations required the organization of police forces or courts or both. Pawnees, Klamaths, Modocs, Navajos, Apaches, Blackfeet, Chippewas, and Sioux were among the tribes involved. At the Pawnee Agency, continued horse thefts led the agent to act. He selected six respected warriors from each of the four bands, uniformed them attractively, and ordered an end to the larceny. Challenged and flattered by the distinction and responsibility, the police proceeded to curtail one of the most popular and prestigious activities of their people. Generations of young Pawnees had demonstrated their right to be called warriors by raiding the horse herds of their enemies. But now when a proud party raced into camp with thirty-four prizes from a herd of the Delawares, the Pawnee police seized and restored the stolen property. They did the same thing with other stock stolen from the army and from settlers.[1] So successful was the force that it survived a change in administration, and the next agent continued the police as a mainstay in preserving order among the Pawnees.

On the Klamath Reservation a new superintendent for the Indians of Oregon was confronted with a tense situation.

1. AR of Benj. F. Lushbaugh, 1862 (ser. 1157, p. 266); George E. Hyde, *Pawnee Indians* (Denver, 1951), p. 190.

John B. Meacham took over the affairs of the Klamaths and their close relatives the Modocs, to find the latter particularly restive and continually slipping off the reservation to return to old haunts. To help contain recalcitrant leaders like Captain Jack and the tribal shamans, Meacham arranged the election of more amenable chiefs and inaugurated a code of laws and a court staffed by the chiefs. The code reflected Anglo-Saxon legal tradition and did particular violence to the Klamath–Modoc sex mores by trying to enforce monogamy and by interfering with a husband's traditional right to take a lodge pole to his wife if she proved obstreperous. Nevertheless, the judges seemed to enjoy their position, and Meacham was soon to complain that the chiefs were making arrests "for trifling offenses or no offenses at all."[2] That they failed in the mission the agent had assigned them, however, was proven by an outbreak two years later in which Meacham was badly wounded and narrowly escaped being scalped by Captain Jack and his fellow conspirators. This was an incident in the nasty little Modoc War fought in the lava beds in northern California.

The Navajo experiment stemmed from a problem similar to that on the Pawnee Reservation. Thought of today as artists in silver and wool, in 1872 the Navajos still bore the reputation of fierce warriors who had raided the Mexican frontier settlements and the Pueblo Indians for as long as tribal memory ran. Defeated and driven into captivity by Colonel Kit Carson in 1863, they had been permitted to return to their home country in 1870. Like the Pawnees, the Navajos had not been completely broken of their wild, free habits, and settlers near their reservations complained incessantly of losing stock. In the hope of stopping the rustlers, a Special Indian Commissioner, General O. O. Howard,

2. Thomas E. Dutelle, "Development of Political Leadership and Institutions Among the Klamath Indians," M.A. Thesis (1951), p. 26.

ordered the recruitment of about a hundred young Navajos
and placed them under the command of the renowned war
chief Manuelito. So effective were they that within six
months their agent proposed reducing the force to thirty
men. A year after it had been raised, the force was officially
disbanded, although it was kept in service briefly by other
financial support. A new agent paid them from the surplus
of annuity goods remaining after the annual issue.

Closely related to the Navajos and sharing their dread
reputation in the 1860s were the Apaches. On one of their
reservations in 1874, according to Agent John P. Clum,
the concept of Indian police *"had its inception."*[3] This categorical statement was made many years later, but there is
basis for the boast because the San Carlos Agency was the
scene of one of the earliest and most successful uses of
Indian police.

In 1873, at the age of twenty-three and only two years
removed from the Rutgers campus, John P. Clum accepted
appointment as agent for the Apaches at San Carlos in
southeastern Arizona. No railroad yet crossed the region,
and its only communication with the outside world was the
overland stage and a single telegraph line maintained by
the army. There could have been few less attractive posts
in the Indian service, but it did not daunt the brash young
Easterner. He was prematurely bald and he concluded that
he did not have much hair to lose to hostile redskins.[4]

Clum's assignment would have intimidated older, more
experienced hands. That he should have been offered the
job at all is indicative of its undesirability and the inefficient
recruiting methods of the Office of Indian Affairs, despite
the inauguration of the "Quaker Policy" by President Grant.

3. John P. Clum, "The San Carlos Indian Police," *New Mexico
Historical Review* (July 1929), p. 203.
4. Woodworth Clum, *Apache Agent* (New York, 1936), p. 128.

This was supposed to eliminate some of the inefficiency and corruption from the Indian Service by transferring the nomination of reservation personnel from the politicians to the various religious denominations. The San Carlos Agency happened to fall to the Dutch Reformed, who also supported Rutgers, and Clum had attended the college briefly. The Reformed Church members entrusted with nominating a new agent included the Rutgers campus in their recruiting area. Presumably Clum got the offer because someone at the college recalled that a former classmate had taken a position with the Signal Corps at Santa Fe.[5] But Clum might have ended as a teacher or with no agency position at all. The Board of Foreign Missions of the Reformed Church was considering him as a teacher or as an agent unless the Indian Office proposed to concentrate most of the Apaches on one Arizona reservation; in that case they had another man in mind. Chosen so casually, young Clum revealed surprising talent for the assignment. The Tucson newspaper announced his appointment with the laconic observation, "We have no knowledge of who Mr. Clum is."[6] By the time Clum had occupied the position for a year, the paper had become totally committed to his support.

Clum stepped into an awkward situation. In 1874 the Apaches in Arizona were divided among four different agencies: Rio Verde, Chiricahua, San Carlos, and Camp Apache, although the last two were considered jointly as the White Mountain Reservation. Officials in Washington were mulling over the advantages of concentrating the populations of Camp Apache, Rio Verde, and San Carlos. There was also considerable dissatisfaction with the role of the

5. J. M. Ferris to Secretary of the Interior, Jan. 8, 1874 (Sec. Interior Appt. File).

6. Tucson, *Arizona Citizen* (March 28, 1874).

military in Apache affairs. General George Crook, commanding the Department of Arizona, was pursuing a policy which appeared to the East to be brutally harsh. The general also seemed to be arrogating to himself all policy-making powers relative to the Apaches, and his attitude was reflected in the subordinate officers stationed at particular agencies. They did not hesitate to overrule local agents whom they seemed to regard as either incompetent or corrupt, and sometimes both. Unfortunately, the general quality of Indian Service personnel admitted of such criticism.

Notified of his appointment as agent at San Carlos, Clum reported to Washington for a briefing on his new post. What the young man heard seems to have shaken his confidence in his ability to handle the agency.[7] Apparently he was told of proposals to concentrate the Apaches and of the troubled relations in Arizona between Indian Service personnel and the army. News from the West that some of his new charges had left the reservation and were burning, killing, and looting nearby could have contributed nothing to his composure. En route to his new assignment Clum was regaled with harrowing details of the murder of whites at San Carlos and of other atrocities committed by his Indians. Purchasing a Colt .45, he prepared himself for a dubious future by improving his pistolry at the expense of the cacti between the village of Tucson and the San Carlos Agency.

On arriving at his post August 8, 1874, the young agent found himself in charge of an area roughly the size of Connecticut, much of it rough, mountainous terrain. A detachment of cavalry was located at San Carlos, and its commanding officer had been making the major decisions despite the presence of a subagent. Indeed, the entire White

7. J. M. Ferris to Sec. of the Interior, Feb. 26, 1874 (Sec. Interior Appt. File).

Mountain Reservation was under military control if the
complaints of Clum's predecessor are to be believed.[8] But
Clum lost no time in reminding the army personnel that he
was in charge and that their role was to aid him—*if* he called
on them. Within a week he had rebuked the local troop
commander for summoning an Indian council in "direct
usurpation of my rights."[9] Two weeks later the agent informed the army officer that in the future if the officer
wished to know the number of Indians at San Carlos he
was not to undertake a personal count but to secure the
information from agency records. John P. Clum intended
to be agent in more than name.

The problem was how Clum, or any other civilian agent,
could control Indians as unruly as the Apaches without
calling on the army. And as had been demonstrated time
and time again, an agent dependent upon troops to maintain
order at his agency soon found the military controlling him
as well. Clum found the answer in Indian police.

The new agent was much impressed by one innovation of
the military. In line with his policy of first punishing the
Indians and then negotiating with them, General Crook had
demanded as a prerequisite to negotiation that renegade
bands bring in the heads of their leaders. Two days after
Clum's arrival at San Carlos, Apaches handed over the
head of a hostile fellow tribesman. Before the end of the
month friendly Indians had brought in another gory trophy
and seventy-six captives.[10] Six heads were brought in that
summer, and not a single white man had accompanied the
Indians on the last sweep. Applying this successful policy
in off-reservation matters to his own problem, Clum ap-

8. James E. Roberts to Commissioner of Indian Affairs (CIA),
July 4, 1874 (OIALR, Roll 11).
9. Clum to Lt. J. B. Babcock, Aug. 15, 1874 (OIALR, Roll 10).
10. Clum to CIA, Aug. 10, 1874, ibid.

pointed four Apache policemen at salaries of $15 per month.[11]

With this minuscule force at his command the agent sought to free his reservation further from military interference. The most he hoped to do immediately was to secure the removal of troops and their "demoralizing" influence from the vicinity of the Indian camps. Their complete removal from the reservation would have to wait, but it came surprisingly fast. Within a month Clum had declared his independence of the military and, more unexpectedly, had obtained their tacit recognition of it. In another thirty days he felt confident enough to request the complete removal of troops from the reservation. He argued that they were no longer needed and, indeed, their continued presence might drive the Indians off. Clum also complained that the military "oppose the Agent and the 'peace policy' in every way possible and seek to defeat every effort of the civil authorities to control the Indians."[12]

Six months after he arrived at San Carlos, Agent Clum had his Indians under good control. They had to attend a daily count and could be absent more than a day only if they had a pass. Clum had all their firearms, and Indians wishing to hunt had to draw weapons at the agency office. So well organized were things at San Carlos that the Indian Office closed the Camp Verde Agency and transferred its Indians to Clum's jurisdiction. The consolidation of the Arizona Apaches at San Carlos had begun.

The next step in the process was to close Camp Apache, and at this point Clum found himself once again at odds with the military. General Crook had been succeeded in command of the Department of Arizona by Colonel August V. Kautz. A West Point classmate of Crook and Phil Sheridan,

11. AR of Clum, 1874 (ser. 1639, p. 605).
12. Clum to CIA, Oct. 16, 1874 (OIALR, Roll 10).

and a long-time friend of Ulysses S. Grant, Kautz must have been surprised to find himself engaged in sharp rivalry with an obscure Indian agent still in his mid-twenties. Reflecting on it later, the officer saw it as part of a conspiracy against him by the "Tucson faction," with the governor and surveyor-general playing leading roles.[13]

By May 1875 the first shot had been fired in a newspaper war in which the military viewpoint was espoused by *The Miner* at Prescott (Kautz's headquarters), with a Tucson journal backing Clum. As tempers rose the Prescott editor leveled charges of incompetence and corruption at Clum. He also voiced the military's belief that the concentration of Indians at San Carlos was for the benefit of Tucson merchants, an "Indian Ring."[14] Clum defended himself in caustic letters to the editor of the Tucson paper, and the editor supported the agent and attacked Kautz for failure to move energetically against Indian renegades. Clum also received valuable backing from the governor of Arizona Territory, A. P. K. Safford.

Stung by Clum's remarks, the military refused to assist the young upstart. When Clum took over Camp Apache, the officer commanding troops denied him "guards or guardhouse."[15] Thus Clum was forced to rely even more heavily on his police. As the Indian population at San Carlos grew, he increased the size of his force proportionately. At the arrival of the Camp Verde Indians, the force was doubled in size to eight, and the addition of the Camp Apache tribesmen saw the number jump to twenty-five. That Clum was still thinking of them primarily as a military force is obvious in his description of their duties. Patrolling and scouting are

13. Entry for Dec. 31, 1877, Diary of Gen. August V. Kautz.

14. For example, see Prescott, *Weekly Miner* (Nov. 17, 1876; April 20, 1877).

15. Clum to CIA, May 1, 1875 (OIALR, Roll 13).

mentioned most frequently, and Clum boasted "the police force has entirely superseded the necessity of a military force."[16] He also established a precedent by choosing as his chief of police a white man. Clay Beauford, a Virginian, was described by Clum as "brave and energetic, a thorough Indian fighter, and when once he strikes a trail he never stops until he is victor in the renegade camp."[17]

Clum was well aware of the significance of the experiment in which he was engaged. In seeking additional funds for his agency he reminded the Indian Commissioner:

We are just testing a delicate question in Indian management—viz. "Can these Indians be controled [sic] by a force of their own." It has been the expressed desire of the Department to have the matter tested, believing that the trial would result in success. . . . The Department cannot afford to hazard too much by an injudicious economy. We must succeed here or the "Peace Policy" in Arizona will be considered an utter failure.[18]

For the first but not the last time, Clum suggested that his resignation might be forthcoming unless he received more support from Washington. From San Carlos it appeared that the Indian Office was endorsing the recruitment of police and permitting the agency to become more dependent on them but then blithely failing to increase the agency's budget to care for the new expense. Clum was not only

16. AR of Clum, 1875 (ser. 1680, p. 718).

17. AR of Clum, 1876 (ser. 1749, p. 416).

18. Clum to CIA, Dec. 13, 1875 (OIALR, Roll 16). Evidence that the Board of Indian Commissioners was interested in Indian police as a substitute for military control is to be seen in an entry for July 28, 1875, in their minutes. It recorded that the board proposed to send a circular letter to the agents soliciting their opinion of such an experiment.

expected to produce the miracle but to pay for it as well from his normal operating budget.

Finances troubled the agent; the loyalty of the police did not. The circumstances surrounding the death of Disalin, a Tonto chief, reassured him on that score. Disalin had been having domestic difficulties and attributed them to advice Clum had given his wives. With a revolver concealed under a shawl draped across his shoulders the Apache went to the agency office determined to reassert his mastery of his household. Entering, Disalin fired at the clerk, then at an Indian near the door, and finally at Chief of Police Beauford, none of the shots taking effect. Alerted by the firing, Indian police ran up, blocked Disalin's escape, and killed him with a volley. One of the policemen was the dead Apache's brother. His quiet, "I have killed my own chief, my own brother; he tried to kill a white man, so we had to kill him," convinced Agent Clum that not even family ties would deter the police from the discharge of duty.[19]

But Clum's critic, *The Miner,* refused to take such an optimistic view of things. Displaying the typical frontier evaluation of Apache personality, *The Miner* suggested:

> The disposition which caused them to kill their chief and brother, to please the agent, can be easily reversed, and should some disaffected and influential Indian take it into his head to get up a mutiny, nothing would please the same Indian police better than to exercise their prowess in brutality by murdering and torturing all the whites within the range of their power.[20]

By late February 1876 Clum had decided to resign, citing

19. Clum to Editor, *Arizona Citizen* (Dec. 27, 1875); Clum to Edward C. Kemble, Dec. 26, 1875 (OIALR, Roll 16).
20. *Weekly Miner* (Jan. 21, 1876).

finances as the reason. He assured the Indian Commissioner: "The main purpose for which I set out has been accomplished; viz, the consolidation of the various tribes of Indians at the Agency, and the inauguration of a policy based on the principles of self-government."[21] But he was to remain at his post for another year and a half, and in that time the value of Indian police was demonstrated beyond the shadow of a doubt. Meanwhile, the young man grew a luxuriant mustache which helped compensate for his receding hairline.

Two incidents illustrate the effectiveness of Clum's Apache force: a scout led by Clay Beauford, and the shackling of Geronimo. Beauford's operation demonstrated the degree to which Clum had freed himself from dependence on the military. When the agent learned of renegade Apaches lurking in a remote area of the reservation, he dispatched Beauford and fifteen police to track them down. Within two weeks the police had located the hostiles, killed sixteen, and returned to base with twenty-one prisoners. Only four hostiles escaped, and one of these was badly wounded.[22]

The Geronimo episode originated in a raid on Arizona settlements by Apaches nominally assigned to the Warm Springs Reservation in New Mexico. Arizona Governor Safford felt that lax supervision by the Warm Springs agent was responsible and urged the Indian Commissioner to discharge him and authorize Clum to move the bands involved to San Carlos. This the Indian Commissioner did, and to accomplish the removal Clum organized a special force of 103 Apache braves. His description of them as "police" is indicative of Clum's casual use of the term. Any Indians bearing arms by his direction and engaged in maintaining law and order on the reservation, or temporarily serving in

21. Clum to CIA, Feb. 26, 1876 (Sec. Interior Appt. File).

22. Clum to Officer Commanding Camp Apache, March 10, 1876 (OIALR, Roll 16).

the territorial militia to run down renegades anywhere in
Arizona or New Mexico, were so designated. Actually the
official reservation force at this time numbered only twenty-
five.

The young agent managed to make this last exploit involving his police a sensational one. Scorning to wait for
the troops made available to him, he entered the Warm
Springs Reservation escorted only by his police. For his test
of strength with Geronimo he devised a neat stratagem.
Clum made the final approach to the agency headquarters
in daylight, accompanied by only twenty-two police. The
remainder of the force he left a few miles out with orders
to come in after nightfall. When the reserves slipped in
they were hidden in a commissary warehouse, leaving the
fifty Apache leaders, presenting themselves at Clum's invita-
tion, under the illusion that they had the agent badly out-
numbered. But as Clum prepared to make his demands, on
signal the doors of the warehouse were flung open, and with
rifles at the ready the reserve raced out to take up positions
commanding the council. Clum then ordered the surrender of
the suspected renegades and disarmed the Apaches. When
Geronimo was called forward to be taken into custody, there
was a tense moment, dissolved when a sergeant of police
snatched Geronimo's knife from his belt as Clay Beauford
covered him with a rifle. To complete Geronimo's humilia-
tion, he and six of his headmen were publicly shackled with
ankle-irons.[23]

Delighted with the coup, the Indian Commissioner altered
Clum's orders to include removal of all the Apache bands at
Warm Springs to San Carlos. Thus another agent had been
relieved and San Carlos' population further swelled. But

23. Clum to Editor, *Arizona Citizen* (May 5, 1877); Clum, *Apache
Agent,* pp. 216 ff.; Clum to CIA, April 21, 1877, and Clum to Maj.
James F. Wade, April 22, 1877 (OIALR, Roll 18).

Clum was not to preside over his empire long. Having withdrawn his resignation, he then resubmitted it and finally turned the agency over to his successor on July 1, 1877. In a last typical bit of bravado he had wired the Commissioner of Indian Affairs that if his salary was increased and he was permitted to raise two additional companies of police, he would "volunteer to take care of all the Apaches in Arizona —the troops can be removed."[24]

On the basis of Clum's figures his police had done a remarkable job, killing or capturing 159 renegades in the mountains as well as keeping the reservation quiet and orderly. With obvious pleasure he noted that "our little squad of Indian Police have done more effective scouting . . . than General Kautz has done with all his troops and four companies of Indian scouts."[25] But Kautz was ably defended by *The Miner* which was by now referring to Clum as the "Gallant Youth" and the "juvenile agent" and uncovering "evidence" of the "Tucson Ring."[26] Their final word of advice was that Clum have his head "banded with iron hoops as a preventitive [sic] to explosion. Where such an extraordinary amount of combined talents exist, mostly composed of gas, there is danger of explosion and death."[27]

Clum's bursts of temper and sensitiveness to criticism were trying to his superiors, but they had borne them gladly because of the young man's other qualities. The agent had received warm praise from the two inspectors the Indian Office had sent to investigate the San Carlos Agency. And these were men whose duty acquainted them with the most sordid episodes afflicting the Indian Service and who were consequently inclined to view things somewhat cynically.

24. Clum to CIA, June 9, 1877 (OIALR, Roll 18).
25. Clum to Editor, *Arizona Citizen* (June 23, 1877).
26. *Weekly Miner* (June 22, 1877).
27. Ibid., June 29, 1877.

Inspector Edward C. Kemble reported that even the military had learned "to desist from interference in the affairs of the Agency."[28] On another occasion Inspector Kemble cited the Disalin episode and his observations at San Carlos as "proof of the efficiency of an Indian Police to maintain order among Indians."[29]

Another inspector had been summoned in the spring of 1877 when Clum's differences with Colonel Kautz came to a head. The colonel had time to devote to the matter since he seldom took the field against the renegades, leaving that chore to subordinates. He did read the territorial papers carefully and, when he was not arbitrating petty feuds among the wives of his staff or worrying about his investments, he presented his views in the friendly *Miner*. In April the colonel took his case directly to Secretary Schurz who assured him that he would have the San Carlos situation investigated.[30]

The Secretary dispatched Inspector William Vandeveer to check the situation, which was disturbing relations between the Departments of War and the Interior and was attracting reporters from as far away as Chicago and San Francisco. Vandeveer supported Clum completely, describing him as having faults, but "the best agent for wild Indians that I know of in the service."[31] He alleged that Clum had been subjected to "persistent and bitter opposition from the military authorities," but, "by the aid of his Indian Police force accomplished far more than [Kautz] with his two regiments of regular soldiers to assist."[32] He termed the agent's innovations in reservation administration a

28. Kemble to CIA, Jan. 7, 1876 (OIALR, Roll 16).
29. Ibid., Jan. 21.
30. Entry for April 21, 1877, Kautz's Diary.
31. Vandeveer to CIA, May 25, 1877 (Sec. Interior Appt. File).
32. Vandeveer to CIA, June 8, 1877 (OIALR, Roll 19).

"signal success" and predicted "the most serious consequences" if a less able man replaced Clum.[33]

Never one to conceal his accomplishments, Clum perhaps provided the best summary of his three years at San Carlos:

> Since taking charge of the San Carlos agency in 1874 it has been my lot to consolidate five agencies into one, and to superintend the movement of about four thousand wild Indians to the San Carlos Reservation; thus bringing together Indians, who by their former locations, were separated by a distance of 600 miles. . . . These movements have all been effected without the loss of a single life, and without destroying the property of citizens.[34]

He had indeed compiled a splendid record, and most of it could be attributed to his agency police, called by his successor "the greatest executive assistance an agent could possible have."[35] John P. Clum was not the only, or even the first, individual to conceive of Indians policing Indians. But his force had undoubtedly been regarded as a test case and had demonstrated conclusively that an Indian agent could achieve relative independence from the military. It encouraged Washington officials to embark on the general experiment.[36]

Officials were receiving additional encouragement from other areas. Chippewas in Wisconsin were inspired by their agent to elect policemen who brought offenders before a tribal court of three old chiefs. An agent at Fort Peck with

33. Vandeveer to CIA, May 25, 1877 (Sec. Interior Appt. File).

34. AR of Clum, 1877 (ser. 1800, p. 431).

35. AR of H. L. Hart, 1878 (ser. 1850, p. 504).

36. In 1877, Commissioner of Indian Affairs E. A. Hayt recommended creation of a police system, arguing: "such a force . . . would, in great measure, relieve the Army from doing police duty on Indian reservations." AR of Hayt, 1877 (ser. 1800, p. 399).

a mixed group of Sioux and Assiniboines reported success, as did the agent for the Blackfeet. The latter was a former city marshal who persuaded his charges to draft an entire code of laws and create a court to enforce it.[37] At the Spotted Tail Agency, Sioux recruited into the army were available as a police force. Their agent surmised that this might be "an auxiliary step toward civilization" and "might be the means of enforcing self-government among the Indians."[38] Elsewhere, agents were complaining of the lack of law enforcement agencies.

In January 1878 on the Kiowa, Comanche, and Wichita Reservation, Agent J. M. Haworth was gloomily anticipating the problems which the end of winter would bring him. "As the cold weather passes away," he wrote the Indian Commissioner, "and the grass begins to grow the number of horse thieves increases." Instead of having to call on the commanding officer at Fort Sill for aid, the agent proposed he be permitted to employ a "police force of Indians to patrol the country." These "would be efficient, not only as far as bad white men, whisky peddlers and horse thieves are concerned but among their own people." Haworth indicated that in the past he had successfully used Indians to arrest Indians.[39] The Commissioner replied that the Office of Indian Affairs had transmitted to the Interior Department a draft of a bill to provide Indian police and hoped Congress would act upon it.[40]

Deluged with proposals for police from personnel in the field, the Indian Commissioners and Secretaries of the Interior had been trying to educate Congressmen in the prob-

37. AR of John S. Wood, 1875 (ser. 1680, p. 802); John C. Ewers, *The Blackfeet* (Norman, 1958), pp. 273–75.
38. AR of J. M. Lee, 1877 (ser. 1800, pp. 466–67).
39. J. M. Haworth to CIA, Jan. 26, 1878 (OIALR, Roll 383).
40. CIA to Haworth, Feb. 7, 1878 (Kiowa Police File).

lems on Indian reservations; they emphasized both the need for law to facilitate the civilization program and the difficulty of simply maintaining order in the Indian country in the absence of law. As Indian Commissioner Edward P. Smith pointed out in 1874:

> No officer of the Government has authority by law for punishing an Indian for crime, or restraining him in any degree; that the only means of enforcing law and order among the tribes is found in the use of the bayonet by the military, or such arbitrary force as the agent may have at his command.[41]

The Trade and Intercourse Act of 1834 was the only general law applicable to the conduct of Indian affairs and it but authorized the agent to expel undesirable individuals.

Off reservation there were additional complications. One Idaho judge held even in 1874 that he had no jurisdiction over a case of murder in his own county, as the crime involved two Indians. The flaw obviously lay in reliance on a statute nearly half a century old, framed, as Commissioner Smith indicated, when the tribes were self-sufficient, and "related to the American Government only as sovereignties." The situation then required only that the Indians:

> be kept as remotely as possible from all settlements, to be assisted as hunters, to be forcibly precluded from an undue supply of gunpowder and rum, and to be kept as peaceable as possible by the presence of an agent and the distribution of a few annuities in cash and blankets.[42]

41. AR of Smith, 1874 (ser. 1639, p. 325).
42. Ibid., pp. 324–25.

The passage of forty years had changed all that. Pushed and pulled by white officials and tribal factions, chiefs were incapable of controlling their own people and completely helpless in the face of harassment from white settlers and reservation hangers-on. The agent normally had no force at his command, and the entire civilization program was suffering. "Year after year we expend millions of dollars for these people in the faint hope that, without law, we can civilize them," another Commissioner Smith complained. "That hope has been," he continued, "to a great degree, a long disappointment; and year after year we repeat the folly of the past."[43]

It was partially to fill a need that the creation of Indian police forces was authorized in May 1878. The Washington administrators would have preferred stronger measures. They had recommended extension of United States laws over all Indian country and provision for enforcement by federal courts. Where the reservation lay within a state, discretionary authority had been proposed to enable the President to place the Indians under jurisdiction of state courts. But these and other measures Congress would not approve. Indeed, the chairman of the House Committee on Indian Affairs also opposed the administration's Indian police scheme.[44] Despite him, Congress accepted an amendment to the appropriation bill for the Indian Service that provided $30,000 for the employment of not over 430 privates and 50 officers. The experiment was underway, and by November 1878, police forces had been organized at about one third of the agencies.[45] The number increased every year. By 1880 two thirds of the agencies had Indian police;[46]

43. AR of J. Q. Smith, 1876 (ser. 1749, p. 388).
44. *Congressional Record,* 10 (3) (1880), 2487.
45. AR of Carl Schurz, 1878 (ser. 1850, p. iv).
46. AR of E. M. Marble, 1880 (ser. 1959, p. 88).

by 1890 there were police at virtually all agencies—a total of 70 officers and 700 privates.[47]

From the beginning their pay, $8 per month for officers and $5 for privates, was a sore point with the Indian police and the agents who had to recruit them. Fringe benefits could include rations for the man and his family if he were stationed on a reservation where the Indians drew rations. He might also receive expense money from an interested citizen for investigating a land dispute, for scouting for the army, or from a tribal council for expelling intruders. Or a special service might be rewarded; for example, a rancher borrowed three policemen to trail rustlers making off with a herd of his horses. For two days of tracking leading to the recovery of the stock, each of the policemen received $10. Even with this type of additional income it was frequently difficult to persuade men to serve, since they were not even furnished mounts. And in situations where they had to carry out extensive patrols of large reservations, two or three horses were needed per man.

Washington received a steady stream of protests on the salary issue. A Sioux agent informed his superiors that on his reservation Indian teamsters who supplied their own horses could earn $30 a month, and $15 was a common wage for reservation jobs that did not entail risking one's life. Where the police were in contact with Indian scouts of the United States Army, their complaints were particularly bitter. The scouts received approximately three times as much pay, were fully equipped when on active duty, and seemed to spend most of their time lounging around, playing cards. Sioux police asked, "Why does not the Great Father pay us for our services the same as he pays the white soldiers? We perform as much duty; we take as many or more risks

47. AR of T. J. Morgan, 1890 (ser. 2841, p. xciv).

of our lives; we arrest and deliver to justice our own friends."[48] Apache police complained that they were being asked to serve for less than the $15 they had originally received, while their fellow tribesmen enrolled as army scouts received $13 per month, a better ration, and a clothing allowance of $4 per month—and did less than half the work.[49]

If the pay scale seemed inadequate to Sioux and Apaches just learning the amenities of civilization, to the more acculturated tribesmen on the Pacific Coast or in eastern Oklahoma it was absurd. Nevertheless, the agents for the Five Civilized Tribes were able to recruit police. They did so by providing duty schedules which permitted Indian policemen to serve also as guards for coal-mining companies and as special agents for railroads, drawing from those sources several times their government salary. They also drew expense money for removing intruders. Confronted with a comparable problem in Washington, the agent at Yakima permitted his police to act as constables when they were located in counties which had justice of the peace courts. To provide adequate pay, agents were known to resort to such questionable practices as placing in a salary fund the fines received by local courts or using the proceeds from sales of confiscated property. Many police must have been rewarded, as were two Mescalero captors of a hostile from Victorio's band, by being permitted to keep the arms and horse of their prisoner. Some agents, to judge from the number of such suggestions received by the Indian Commissioner, possibly hired fewer police than were authorized and used the padded payroll to increase the wages of those actually on duty.

Despite the volume of complaints from the field, the

48. AR of J. Cook, 1880 (ser. 1959, p. 168).
49. J. H. Hammond to CIA, July 24, 1879 (OIALR, Roll 23).

repeated requests from secretaries and commissioners, and the resignation for pay reasons of about 16 per cent of the police in a single year, not until 1885 did Congress authorize paltry raises of $2 a month for officers and $3 for privates.[50] As there was no increase in the total appropriation, even this pittance was made possible only by cutting the total number of police. To top it off, the bill eliminated rations for families of policemen. This more than offset the raises in certain situations, and more police resigned. As the protests mounted, improvements came slowly. There were raises first to $12 for officers and $10 for privates, then to $15 for officers but no increase for the privates. By 1906 officers earned only $25 and privates $20.

Uniforms were also a touchy subject with police and agents. It was several years before the uniform was standardized, and agents originally were authorized to purchase what they needed, or they were issued whatever was available. The same Sioux who complained in 1880 about their pay disliked their uniforms—gray ones left over from those worn by guards at the Centennial Exposition. "Why does he clothe us in the dress and uniform of the Great Father's late enemies?" the Indians asked. "Why does he require us to wear a gray uniform when all his other soldiers wear blue?"[51] Blue it was finally—blue trousers, a darker blue slouch hat, and gold-buttoned, dark blue blouse, the latter bearing a badge. The officer's badge was star-shaped, but a plain shield sufficed for the privates. Earlier models had been shields with stars across the top to signify rank. The officers might also sport shoulder tabs.

The uniforms were not tailored and frequently fitted badly. Utes were not tall but were very broad-chested, and their agent said if he did not receive larger uniforms he

50. AR of H. Price, 1884 (ser. 2287, p. 13).
51. AR of J. Cook, 1880 (ser. 1959, p. 168).

would have to discharge his present force and hire smaller men. The handkerchiefs the Utes and other Indians wore inside their collars, and other nonregulation innovations like moccasins, did not add much. But when the stranger on the reservation first confronted a policeman, he could be impressed. Writing in the 1930s, anthropologist Clark Wissler who had frequented reservations around the turn of the century, recollected best the police weapons:

> The essential lines in the picture were defined by an oversized six-shooter, a heavy broad leather belt full of shells, and an enormous black hat. A repeating rifle usually swung from the saddle. In short, one's first impression of an Indian policeman might include little more than heavy armament and a poker face.[52]

This "heavy armament" was yet another bone of contention. Strangely, there was no initial provision for arming the police. The white chief of police for the Mescalero Apaches complained of having to buy ammunition from his own pocket because otherwise, when he carried government funds, he was escorted by police without "arms in their hands and something to put in them to make a noise with."[53] To train his Kiowa and Comanche policemen their agent tried to borrow rifles and a copy of Upton's *Tactics* from neighboring Fort Sill. To evict trespassing cattlemen his unarmed police themselves required an escort of cavalry from the army post. On another occasion the weapons situation led to a curious official explanation for ammunition expenditure: "Some of this ammunition was also issued to the Indian Police when it *suited such arms as they might be*

52. Clark Wissler, *Indian Cavalcade* (New York, 1938), p. 118.
53. James L. Smith to Mescalero Agent, July 1, 1882 (Mescalero Agency File).

able to pick up when starting out on an expedition."[54] Not until the summer of 1880 did these police receive weapons, and then only rifles. Two years later the Kiowa and Comanche agent was complaining that they were "nearly all in unserviceable condition for want of slight repairs, and no fixed ammunition having been issued to them for two years or more."[55] Nevertheless, the agent was now forced to plead that these undependable weapons, at least badges of authority, should not be taken from them until revolvers arrived.

Secretary of the Interior Henry M. Teller was a Coloradan who had had personal experience with hostile Indians, and he, on occasion, manifested all the hate and fear usually engendered in frontiersmen by Indians. Like other frontiersmen, however, he was not averse to making a quick buck at Indian expense, as he later demonstrated when dealing with the Kickapoo in his official capacity as a United States senator.[56]

In 1882, Secretary Teller decided that revolvers should replace the long-range rifles in the hands of the police, the revolvers to be purchased, incidentally, by savings made possible by temporary cuts in the number of police. So alarmed was Teller at the thought of rifle-bearing Indians that he insisted these weapons be taken up even before the arrival of the revolvers. The prospect of exchanging rifles for revolvers dampened police morale. The Cheyenne and Arapaho agent commented bitterly that his police, so armed and trying to arrest desperate men equipped with rifles, "Had about as well take clubs."[57] And the revolvers either arrived in poor condition or suffered from poor maintenance. In

54. P. B. Hunt to CIA, April 19, 1880 (OIALR, Roll 386); italics are mine.

55. P. B. Hunt to CIA, Oct. 6, 1882 (OIALR, 18499, 1882).

56. A. M. Gibson, *The Kickapoos* (Norman, 1963), pp. 351–54.

57. Jno. D. Miles to Kiowa Agent, Oct. 13, 1882 (Kiowa Police File).

following years one agent complained that his force had
no carbines, only five of the thirty-three revolvers at his
agency would fire, and "the lawless element . . . are fully
aware of this state of facts, and take advantage of them."[58]
A cavalry officer acting as a Sioux agent ridiculed as a
"farce" the faulty revolvers issued to his police. He scoffed:
"The idea of ordering a man so armed to arrest a mad
Indian who wants to die, but wants to kill as many people
as he can before going, and one armed with a Winchester
rifle!"[59] Obviously the effective weapons contemporaries
saw in the hands of police were either their own or the special
exceptions the Indian Commissioner referred to in a letter
to a complaining agent in 1893. Until the late 1890s, the
general policy Secretary Teller had laid down of refusing
to issue rifles or fixed ammunition, except for slaughtering
cattle, was adhered to. When it was finally relaxed, the
police on one reservation also received billy clubs!

Pistols that wouldn't fire, starvation wages, and shoddy
uniforms all complicated recruiting. The agent directed to
organize a police force of a specified size—they ranged in
1890 from two to forty-three—might also have to contend
with the opposition of a chief who recognized a threat to
his authority. And not just any recruit would do. Agents
sought Indians who would command respect within the
tribe and had the mental and physical qualifications to discharge arduous and potentially dangerous duty. Progressives
—Indians displaying a willingness to adapt to the white
man's ways—were preferred to the traditionalists, the Conservatives.[60] The Dawes Severalty Act of 1887 specified that

58. J. Lee Hall to CIA, Nov. 19, 1885 (OIALR, 28025, 1885).

59. AR of W. A. Sprole, 1893 (ser. 3210, p. 191).

60. Throughout this study the terms Progressive and Conservative
are used to designate two ubiquitous tribal factions. The amenable and
cooperative Progressive who was willing to adapt to the white man's

preference for police appointments should go to those who
had received allotments. This introduced a new complica-
tion; the Progressive who worked his own land could not
afford to take on a job with such miserable pay. Discharged
army scouts were the answer for one agent.[61] Another stout-
hearted one turned to recent Cheyenne hostiles who had
undergone rehabilitation in Florida, and Little Medicine,
Antelope, Left Hand, and their fellow ex-prisoners performed faithfully.[62] But overriding all other requirements
was the necessity of having a force representative of the
several bands or tribes on the reservation. At one agency this
required including on a fourteen-man force two Peorias,
three Senecas, three Wyandottes, two Modocs, one Quapaw,
two Ottawas, and one Miami![63] They must have required
interpreters to communicate among themselves, though it is
likely that they seldom were called out as a unit.

There were innumerable duty systems employed, a common one being to station a policeman or two with each
important band on the reservation. This made it difficult
to train them effectively or to develop esprit de corps. Profit-
ing from the army's experience with Indian scouts, some
agents selected as chief of police and drillmaster a member
of the agency staff with military experience. Where unit
training and common housing and messing facilities were
available, the police developed into quite effective paramilitary organizations. As was to be expected, the nature of
their duties did not add to their popularity. "The police are

way was favored by the Indian Service personnel. The Conservative who
clung to his blanket (he was the "blanket" Indian) and his other native
ways was more popular with his fellow Indians.

61. AR of J. Geo. Wright, 1894 (ser. 3306, p. 296).
62. AR of J. D. Miles, 1878 (ser. 1850, p. 551).
63. Descriptive Statement of Proposed Changes in the Indian Police
Force at Quapaw Agency (Quapaw Police File).

looked upon as a common foe, and the multitude are bitterly opposed to them," observed one white official.[64] But what was an index of their unpopularity with their fellow tribesman was an index of their usefulness to the agent.

The Indian police had appeared in response to a crying need on reservations in the post-Civil War era. The need is attested by the number of agents who experimented with police during the 1860s and 1870s. If the Peace Policy, whose aim was not to exterminate the red man but rather to lead him down the white man's road, were to succeed, the administrators had to devise some way to eliminate military interference with the reservation populations. A well-equipped and disciplined Indian police force could be the answer. But after John Clum proved the merit of the policy, the Commissioners of Indian Affairs learned quickly that it was one thing to devise such a policy and another to persuade Congress to appropriate sufficient funds to implement it. Economy-minded congressmen were reinforced by colleagues who constituted an army lobby and had no interest in seeing an Indian police system work. Nevertheless, the poorly paid and equipped Indian police soon made themselves indispensable as reservation handymen, law officers, and agents of the civilization process.

64. AR of John L. Gasmann, 1885 (ser. 2379, p. 248).

3. Law Officers and Reservation Handymen

THE INDIAN POLICEMAN was the reservation handyman. He performed housekeeping duties on the reservation, tried to preserve law and order, and served as an agent of the civilization program. Maintenance and housekeeping occupied most of his time: he supplemented the agent's labor force by cleaning out irrigation ditches, killing beef cattle for the meat ration, taking the census, building roads, carrying messages, and performing a dozen other chores. Such routine assignments may not have been exciting, but they contributed measurably to the efficiency of reservation administration and lengthened the lives of agents.

To be effective, the agent first had to know what was going on. In consideration of his almost certain inability to speak the language of his charges, together with the size of his domain, this was not simple, but the police were satisfactory liaison agents. They checked on the squaw men, reported white intruders, and kept the agent abreast of the tribe's factional squabbles. As the eyes and ears of the agent, the police enabled him to forestall trouble which otherwise might have burgeoned into first-class difficulties requiring the intervention of cavalry and Gatling guns.

How varied were the tasks facing the police can be seen in the entries in a log maintained by the captain of police on the Quapaw Reservation in the summer and fall of 1878.

They reveal that he spent much of his time trying to prevent settlers from looting the reservation's natural resources. These scroungers cut timber, gathered sixteen wagonloads of hickory nuts, fished, hunted, and stole horses. On July 18 the policeman was "out after a lightening Rod man for not paying his board." August 10 he was "out all night and captured wrong men and turn[ed] them loose." On another occasion he received orders to "help Julia Valley get her household goods" in what must have been a domestic dispute.[1]

In different areas of the Indian country the emphasis of police activity varied. Among the Apaches and the recently hostile Sioux, police helped keep the dissidents under control and ran down renegades. On the reservations in western Oklahoma the principal problem was preventing white ranchers from grazing their herds on Indian grass. Farther east, poachers and timber cutters competed with thieves and murderers for the attention of the police. Everywhere bootleggers and moonshiners presented a never-ending problem.

Keeping Indian pastures free of white ranchers' cattle was not a glamorous duty but a continuous and perplexing job. Texas cattlemen, gazing across the Red River at the nearly vacant pastures of the four million acres of the Kiowa, Comanche, and Wichita Reservation devised both legal and illegal methods of fattening their stock on Indian grass. The legal way was to negotiate a lease, a practice which itself led to considerable corruption as the Texans competed with each other for tribal favor and the most profitable deal possible. The illegal technique was simply to drive cattle onto the reservation and leave them there until they were detected and removed. In 1882 coping with the Texans was "rapidly becoming the principal business" of the Kiowa and

1. Report Book (Quapaw Police File).

Comanche police.[2] Once they located the herd, they had to count it and list the brands before driving it off Indian land. The information would then be passed through official channels, and ultimately the tribe might collect damages of $1 per head. If the herd had grazed long enough, however, the rancher would profit even if he paid damages. Some seem to have gambled on this possibility. Or they might "buy up the policemen," as an inspector reported they were probably doing.[3] Some idea of the magnitude of the grazing problem is seen in the removal from the Kiowa and Comanche land of over 10,000 head of Texas cattle in the summer of 1886 alone.[4]

Nor was the problem peculiar to the Southwest. Yakima police in Washington resigned in protest at the miserable compensation for the unending job of guarding a line forty miles long, deliberately near which white men grazed their cattle and sheep. Hogs turned out by white settlers to forage for themselves were problems elsewhere.

Cattle rustlers and horse thieves seem to have had even less respect for property of Indians than for that of white men. Undoubtedly, running off Indian stock was easier, and less likely to result in a prison sentence or the noose, than violating the property rights of whites. Judge Parker summarized the attitude of many of his fellow citizens in his observation on those who cut Indian timber: "A class of men . . . who revel in the idea that they have an inherent, natural right to steal from the Indians."[5] Even walnuts and hickory nuts brought out the thievish proclivities of frontiersmen, as the police captain reported. Game on Indian land

2. P. B. Hunt to CIA, Jan. 24, 1882, in Martha Buntin, "Beginning of the Leasing of the Surplus Grazing Lands," *Chronicles of Oklahoma* (Sept. 1932), p. 370.

3. W. W. Jenkins to CIA, June 28, 1890 (OIALR, 22268, 1890).

4. AR of J. Lee Hall, 1886 (ser. 2467, p. 349).

5. Harrington, *Hanging Judge,* p. 172.

in eastern Oklahoma attracted not only sportsmen willing to ignore Indian rights for a little recreation but hunters who made a business of it. Thousands of quail and prairie chickens were slaughtered or netted and shipped to Saint Louis and Kansas City. One policeman confiscated and then released 114 dozen quail addressed to New Zealand![6] Trying to keep this type of poaching at a minimum occupied much police time.

Alcohol in one form or another provided tribal police with more serious problems, sometimes as a result of their own inability to handle it. One agent observed caustically, "The first indication of a whiskey peddler is usually a drunken police."[7] Another entire force, while on a mission to protect settlers from Apaches, found liquor and dissolved into a "drunken mob" after learning of a government decision not to issue them rations.[8] But most policemen managed to resist temptation, whether it came in the form of straight whiskey or in more exotic forms such as patent medicine, Choctaw beer, or tiswin, the last being a potent corn brew popular with Indians of the Southwest.

Drunken Indians seem to have been responsible for a majority of the crimes committed by their people. Most Indian technologies were not sufficiently sophisticated to produce intoxicants and, as a result, their cultures were even less experienced and less successful in coping with alcoholism than were those of the whites. At one reservation only fifteen crimes were recorded for the year, but three of these were murders and in all instances the guilty Indian was drunk.[9] A Fort Smith grand jury dealing principally with

6. Capt. J. W. Ellis to Agt. Shoenfelt, Aug. 5, 1900 (ser. 4102, p. 243).
7. AR of Samuel L. Patrick, 1890 (ser. 2841, p. 201).
8. AR of R.G. Wheeler, 1882 (ser. 2100, p. 67).
9. AR of John O'Keane, 1880 (ser. 1959, p. 288).

crimes committed in Indian country estimated that 95 per cent of them were attributable to alcohol.[10] Temperance advocates could have found abundant ammunition in conditions in the Indian country.

Some idea of the scope of the problem is apparent in police reports. The Apache force at San Carlos destroyed an estimated 2,000 gallons of tiswin in one year[11]—a large amount for the parched Southwest but nothing compared to the amount confiscated in wetter eastern Oklahoma. To supplement the local production of intoxicants, whiskey peddlers imported whiskey and wine hidden in legitimate freight such as casks of pottery. It also came in as patent medicine under a variety of names. In one month police of the Five Civilized Tribes destroyed over 5,000 gallons of intoxicating liquors, and a single policeman claimed to have spilled as much as 100 gallons in a day.[12]

That it was not all dumped was recalled by an early settler. He told of accompanying an Indian policeman to a railroad depot in an Oklahoma town to confiscate two jugs of whiskey, one of which they proposed to break on the rails. The policeman suggested taking the other jug to a room behind the local Masonic Hall and sharing it with a convivial United States marshal and a couple of thirsty carpenters. Having verified the contents of the jugs by prolonged sipping, they were about to break the one on the rails when an elderly Negro pleaded for a drink. But when the jug was passed to him for a swallow, it took both the settler and the policeman to separate the old man from it. Then having broken that jug and watched the contents seep into the ground, they prepared to retire to the room behind

10. AR of Leo E. Bennett, 1889 (ser. 2725, p. 210).

11. AR of J. C. Tiffany, 1881 (ser. 2018, p. 67).

12. AR of Leo E. Bennett, 1889 (ser. 2725, p. 210); Ellis to Shoenfelt (n. 6 above).

the Masonic Hall for their party, only to discover that in the confusion someone had swiped the second jug! And to make it a complete disaster the white man had almost cut off two fingers in the process of breaking the jug.[13]

That incident had its humorous aspects, but others were more typical of the problems of the police with alcohol. At the Cheyenne and Arapaho Agency in 1888 "Whiskey Jim" was notorious for supplying the alcoholics among the Indians and troops. When finally cornered by Lieutenant Coyote and Private Sleeping Wolf, he put up a fierce struggle, and all three men were badly wounded before he was on his way to a year in the penitentiary.

Mortal wounds were incurred by Indian policemen in a variety of situations. A member of the Klamath force died at the hands of a drunken half-blood and his equally intoxicated Indian companion; an Osage was killed by a prisoner he was bringing in; on the streets of Kiowa, Oklahoma, a Choctaw policeman was killed by a local tough who shot him five times and then escaped by playing drunk.

When the tables were turned and the police got their man, there was sometimes a problem of disposal. At the Kiowa Agency a Negro, Monroe Barrett, rode from a store with a new saddle and boots without the formality of paying for them. He was trailed by the police chief Frank Farrell and Pewo, one of his Indian privates. Overtaking Barrett when he stopped for water, Pewo grappled with him; the Negro grabbed Pewo's revolver and got one shot off at Farrell while using Pewo as a shield. But Farrell was a good man with a gun, and he managed to kill the thief. The stolen goods were then returned, but the summer heat made disposal of the corpse a real emergency. The agent met it by a telegram to Barrett's relatives at Chickasha:

13. Grant Foreman, "Indian-Pioneer History," Oklahoma Historical Society MSS., vol. 6, p. 446.

Monroe Barrett was just killed by my Chief of Police while resisting arrest: you are instructed to immediately notify me what disposition to make of the body, and it should be taken care of at the earliest possible moment, owing to the weather conditions.[14]

Such problems must have arisen with particular frequency in eastern Oklahoma. Not only did an occasional drunk resist arrest, but the horse thieves and train robbers who abounded in the area did not hesitate to shoot to kill when apprehended by Indian policemen. Since large-scale stock rustling and train robbery were profitable, outlaw gangs appeared which terrorized the local inhabitants. The Daltons, Starrs, and Cooks, three of the best-known combinations, had several brushes with the police of the Union Agency of the Five Civilized Tribes.

Bob Dalton had once served as a United States deputy marshal and as chief of the Osage police. He lost these positions when he and his younger brother Emmett were exposed as bootleggers. With other members of their family they then graduated to train and bank robbery. An agent for the Five Civilized Tribes protested that, considering the state of their weapons, to send his police after the Daltons was to send them to their death. Two years later his successor was worrying about the Cook Gang, the Daltons having been shot up in the famous daylight robbery of two Coffeyville banks.

Bill Cook, a young mixed-blood Cherokee, led a band of outlaws who defied the law enforcement officers of eastern Oklahoma. Merchants curtailed their operations and trains were under guard and ran only intermittently. The agent ordered all forty-odd of his police to do their duty:

14. Martha Buntin, "History of the Kiowa, Comanche, and Wichita Indian Agency" (M.A. Thesis [1931], p. 127).

Arrest all outlaws, thieves, and murderers in your section, and if they resist you will shoot them on the spot.
And you will aid and assist all deputy United States
marshals in the enforcement of the law, and make
yourselves a terror to evil doers.

If you are afraid to carry out this order, send in your
resignations and I will appoint better men in your
places. This is no time for cravens and cowards to hold
official positions and wear the badges of office.[15]

The order was clear and categorical, but more easily dictated than executed. The Cooks continued to rob railroad
depots, travelers, stores, and a post office. Their most sensational coup was to sidetrack a Kansas City and Missouri
Pacific train and loot the express car and the passengers. By
late October 1895 rumor had it that the Cooks were threatening to take over the town of Claremore. The agent for the
Five Civilized Tribes telegraphed Washington: "My police
force is not equal to the emergency."[16] Within a few weeks,
however, the peace officers had the upper hand, and Bill
Cook had fled the territory. When he returned to it in irons
to stand trial, his gang had dissolved. Under pressure from
several hundred Indian police, marshals, and railroad detec-
tives, the members had fled the country, been shot down, or
were under arrest and awaiting trial before the dread Judge
Parker.

The Indian police of Union Agency, in the face of organized crime of the scope of the Cook Gang, sometimes
looked futile, but in the more normal course of events their
performance was impressive. As Clark Wissler had noted
in their Plains counterparts, they tended to discharge their
duty without fanfare and make only the most laconic re-

15. AR of Dew M. Wisdom, 1895 (ser. 3382, p. 157).
16. Shirley, *Law West of Fort Smith*, p. 112.

ports. In Wissler's example a policeman was ordered to bring in a troublemaking squaw man "dead or alive." Finding the suspect already dead at the hands of another Indian, the policeman adhered strictly to his orders and loaded the corpse on a wagon and brought it in.[17] In the same vein, an agent for the Five Civilized Tribes offered the following as a typical report:

> Dear Sir: Burglars robbed Overstreet's store last night. I followed 'em and killed one. Yours, truly.[18]

Of the scores of men who served on the police force of Union Agency, none was more famous than Captain Sam Sixkiller, a mixed-blood Cherokee who was shot down in the streets of Muskogee in 1886. The son of Redbird Sixkiller and Pamelia Whaley Sixkiller, Sam's two maternal grandparents were white; one parental grandparent was full-blood Cherokee, the other half-blood Cherokee.

Born in Going Snake District of the Cherokee Nation and educated at a Baptist mission, Sam was nineteen years old when the Civil War broke out. His father joined the Union army, and Sam was left to care for the home place. Nevertheless, when some of his neighbors left to enter the Confederate ranks, the young man elected to accompany them. Presumably there was no emotional commitment to the Southern cause, for within a year, without ever having seen combat, he deserted. Slipping north to Fort Gibson, he enlisted in a Union artillery company commanded by his father, now First Lieutenant Redbird Sixkiller. He also failed to see action with the North.

After the war Sam Sixkiller married and moved to Tahlequah, where he worked at odd jobs and farmed until he was appointed High Sheriff in 1875. Sheriff Sixkiller was

17. Wissler, *Indian Cavalcade*, p. 120.
18. AR of Robt. L. Owen, 1888 (ser. 2637, p. 130).

responsible for good order in Tahlequah, the Cherokee
capital. He also served as warden of the national prison,
a large sandstone building just opened and evidence of the
evolution, from corporal punishment to detention, of Cherokee techniques for penalizing criminals.

Like his father, then serving as a justice of the Cherokee
Supreme Court, the son was well liked and respected. A
rather short, stocky man, whose dark skin suggested his
Indian forebears, Sam Sixkiller discharged his routine duties
as warden and sheriff in an exemplary manner. But in
November 1878 his zeal for curtailing rowdyism in the
streets of Tahlequah proved his undoing. Some young Cherokees were riding through the capital whooping, firing their
pistols, and generally disturbing the peace. The high sheriff
and his deputies ran them out of town, but the young ruffians
refused to halt on command and, instead, sent bullets flying
around the law officers. The latter returned the volley and
one of the young men, Jeter T. Thompson, was killed. Before
he died Thompson accused the high sheriff of firing to kill
because of a grudge Sam held against him. The deceased's
family pressed for prosecution of Sixkiller, and Sam was
suspended from his position and charged with murder. The
jury failed to reach a decision, and in retrial he was found
innocent.

Even though cleared by the jury, Sixkiller found it impossible to continue as high sheriff and moved on to Muskogee, capital of the Creek Nation. In February 1880 he became captain of the Union Agency police. He also served
concurrently as a United States deputy marshal and as a
special agent for the Missouri Pacific Railroad. In this last
capacity he earned about $1,200 a year, which far exceeded
his income from the other posts. He was best known, however, as captain of the Union Agency police, and the agent
for the Five Civilized Tribes considered that he faithfully

discharged that duty, whatever his other obligations might have been.

As top man of the Union Agency force Sixkiller had thirty to forty men under him. His principal responsibility, Muskogee, was a frontier town typical of the Indian Territory in the 1880s. It contained a few score buildings, most of them frame, with the business establishments presenting the characteristic false fronts of that day. Except for those lining the railroad tracks, the buildings were scattered about in no particular pattern on a bare prairie whose monotony was unrelieved by shrubs or trees. The arrival of the railroad in 1872 had given the struggling community its reason for being, since it now served as a cattle-shipping and supply center for the ranchers and farmers of the vicinity. There were only about 500 people in Muskogee when the Sixkillers moved there, but as it grew, little was done to improve the village's appearance. The streets remained unpaved, and as late as 1893 they were described as "a mud-hole and hog-wallow" producing "a stench that may cause sickness."[19]

The shabby little village included all the unsavory elements attracted to Indian Territory, but Sam made his influence felt in Muskogee immediately. Within days of his arrival the local *Indian Journal* reported happily: "The Indian police . . . have finally succeeded in making [Muskogee] as quiet and peaceful as Tahlequah."[20] Sixkiller's reputation bore up well in a difficult situation. Four years after he took office, a newspaper in a neighboring town referred to him as "highly respected," a man who "may be safely relied on at all times, whether at the festive board or in a rough-and-tumble, when coolness and decision are desirable qualities."[21]

19. Muskogee *Phoenix* (June 8, 1893), quoted in Grant Foreman, *Muskogee* (Norman, 1943), p. 92.

20. Muskogee, *Indian Journal* (Feb. 12, 1880).

21. Vinita, *Indian Chieftain* (April 24, 1884).

Sixkiller's duties in Muskogee and throughout Union Agency brought him into contact with the most dangerous characters in a society which proliferated them. Although involved in many shootings, in six years' duty with the Indian police he is known definitely to have killed only two men. A target himself on many occasions, he was hit just once prior to his fatal encounter.

The first man the captain killed was a bootlegger who reached for his shotgun, but Sam was faster with his pistol. Bootleggers also precipitated another brisk gun battle; this time they were led by the notorious Negro outlaw Dick Glass. Originally a resident of the Creek Nation, Glass's crimes had made him so unpopular there that he had moved on. Early in June 1885 Captain Sixkiller was informed that Glass and three companions had been seen returning from south of the Red River with a wagonload of Texas whiskey. Accompanied by four other policemen and a guide, Sam laid an ambush. The outlaws entered it, one driving the covered wagon and Glass and the other two walking behind it. Suddenly Sixkiller sprang into the road about ten feet ahead of the horses and called on Glass and his henchmen to surrender. Their answer was to draw their weapons and scatter. As the police opened fire, the driver collapsed and two of the outlaws trailing the wagon died immediately. Glass, one of them, went down from shotgun blasts and slugs from a Winchester. The third man walking at the rear of the wagon took off only to be captured after a short chase. When the police returned to the site of the ambush, they found that the driver, despite his wound, had unhitched the team and ridden off. Harnessed together, the horses could not make good time, and Sam and his men soon overtook the fugitive, accounting for all the outlaws.[22]

22. Ibid., June 11, 1885.

Whiskey, taken aboard by mixed-blood Black Hoyt and a white man, Jess Nicholson, helped set the stage for what a reporter called a "lively little scrimmage" in Muskogee in September 1886.[23] A concert had been scheduled for that evening but was canceled when music lovers feared to leave their homes. Hoyt and Nicholson, their spirits enlivened by "Muskogee water," were firing their pistols in the village streets and generally making nuisances of themselves. Captain Sixkiller and another policeman tried to bring them under control and in the process set themselves up as targets. In spite of their condition the roughs managed to inflict a slight wound in Sam's arm. Before they were subdued, Nicholson had been badly wounded in the foot. Nevertheless, he escaped; Hoyt was jailed. On hearing of his son's imprisonment, Milo Hoyt began to threaten Sixkiller. The father was then arrested and charged with trying to kill the policeman, riotous conduct, and carrying deadly weapons. Meanwhile, Nicholson had taken refuge in the home of another mixed-blood Cherokee, Dick Vann, recently pardoned after being convicted of assault with intent to kill. When a policeman arrived to seize Nicholson, Vann drew a pistol on him and forced him to retreat. Although he avoided jail, Nicholson subsequently died of his wounds, and his friends held Sixkiller responsible.

The explanation for their conduct that Black Hoyt and Nicholson offered was indicative of the temper of the times and the anomalous position occupied by the Indian police in the territory of the Five Civilized Tribes. The men were charged with having fired on deputy marshals, both the policemen holding these commissions. But Hoyt and Nichol-

23. Robert L. Owen to CIA, Sept. 17, 1886 (OIALR, 26546, 1886); AR of Owen, 1886 (ser. 2467, p. 378); Vinita, *Indian Chieftain* (Sept. 23, 1886).

son protested that they were "just shooting at Police." The agent for the Five Civilized Tribes requested legislation to outlaw this frivolous pastime. He also complained of the presence in the community of:

> women of the "baser sort," plying their vocation, and their houses are often the rendezvous of reckless men, who carry deadly weapons, and who become involved in broils, and shoot off their pistols, and terrorize the neighborhoods.[24]

The death of Nicholson possibly led to the slaying of Sam Sixkiller three months later.[25] Some Muskogee residents helped celebrate the Christmas season by staging horse races December 23–24 which attracted to the Creek capital more than the usual quota of hoodlums. Whiskey was flowing quite freely on Christmas Eve, and two racing fans who had downed their share were Alf Cunningham and Dick Vann, the same Vann who had aided Jess Nicholson to escape. Nicholson had since died from his wound, and his buddy Vann was not in a friendly mood.

Cunningham, a mixed-blood Cherokee and Vann's brother-in-law, also was feeling antagonistic toward peace officers. Loitering in town after the race, he had pulled a gun on Creek Lighthorseman Tom Kennard, a descendant of Negro slaves once owned by the Creeks, who happened to be standing in the door of the Commercial Hotel. Kennard was saved by someone who grabbed Cunningham's pistol, giving

24. Owen to CIA (n. 23 above).

25. The account of Sixkiller's death is based on: Muskogee, *Indian Journal* (Dec. 29, 1886); Vinita, *Indian Chieftain* (Dec. 30, 1886); Robert L. Owen to CIA, Dec. 29, 1886 (OIALR, 100, 1887); transcript of *U.S.* v. *Alfred Cunningham* (Creek Foreign Relations File); interview with Mrs. Samuel R. Sixkiller.

the officer an opportunity to draw his own weapon, crash it against his assailant's skull, and disarm him. Unfortunately, Kennard failed to jail Cunningham, and Alf was still walking the streets later that evening. Many good citizens refused to venture out, but Cunningham joined forces with his brother-in-law. Together they attempted to buy a pistol and were refused. Then they swaggered into a hotel where Alf seized a shotgun. Now armed, the two jumped the city marshal, Shelly Keys, who happened by. As a crowd gathered they contented themselves with taking his pistol. Emboldened by the pistol and shotgun, they looked around for Kennard, the Lighthorseman. By chance they ran into Captain Sam Sixkiller first.

That evening Captain Sixkiller had planned to take his children to see the Christmas tree at the Methodist Church. But, suffering from a headache, he first sought relief at the drugstore operated by Dr. M. F. Williams in the Muskogee business district. Sam was unarmed and presumably unaware of the trouble already caused by the Cherokee mixed-bloods, when two men stepped out of the darkness and one of them called him by name. As he walked toward them Vann yelled "You'd never do that to me again," and both of them leveled their weapons at the captain. Apparently Sixkiller got close enough to knock Cunningham's shotgun aside, since the charge of buckshot only riddled his clothes. Vann was more deadly with the pistol. He put four .45 slugs into the policeman, and as Sixkiller fell to the ground he added another. It was all over in a matter of seconds. One of the murderers bent over his victim momentarily, and then they both ran to their horses, mounted, and galloped out of town.

They might have walked, or even remained in Muskogee, for no pursuit materialized. Other law officers chose discretion and remained out of sight. Marshal Keys "changed his coat and hat that he might conceal his identity and looked as though he might like to contract for a cast iron suit of clothes," a reporter observed sardonically.[26]

Sam Sixkiller's death was a severe loss to the community, testified to by doleful and outraged editorial comment and the most impressive funeral yet accorded anyone in Indian Territory.[27] Two thousand turned out to mourn the law officer described as fearless, conscientious, and devoted to his duty. "That a man with so little thought of danger should fall by violence seemed in no way strange," one editor lamented.[28] Indian Agent Robert L. Owen, himself a Cherokee citizen, praised the dead man to the Commissioner of Indian Affairs:

> Saml. Sixkiller died a martyr to the cause of law and order and had the respect and confidence of all the decent people in the country particularly of Hon I. C. Parker, U. S. Judge of this District, M. H. Iandels, Pros. Atty., John Carroll, U. S. Marshall. Every newspaper in the territory had the most respectful and complimentary notices of him.[29]

Richard Vann and Alfred Cunningham were never brought to trial for the murder of Sam Sixkiller. The labyrinth of conflicting jurisdictions in Indian Territory proved to be a staunch ally of the killers. Both were indicted by a Creek court, but the fugitives were in the Cherokee Nation, and that required extradition. Creek Chief J. M. Perryman formally requested custody of the two men from Cherokee Chief D. W. Bushyhead, but before the requisition could be honored, Dick Vann was killed in another burst of gunfire in Fort Gibson. Alf Cunningham's case was com-

26. Vinita, *Indian Chieftain* (Dec. 30, 1886).
27. Tahlequah, *Cherokee Advocate* (Jan. 5, 1887).
28. Vinita, *Indian Chieftain* (Dec. 30, 1886).
29. Robert L. Owen to CIA, Jan. 17, 1887 (OIALR, 1939, 1887).

plicated by the fact that some time after the killing in Muskogee, marshals of Judge Parker's court had taken him to Fort Smith on a larceny charge. This led to extensive correspondence between the federal judge and the two chiefs, since Parker would release Cunningham to Bushyhead only if the Cherokee chief would agree to return him if he were acquitted of the murder charge. And this, of course, required agreement between Bushyhead and Perryman. Parker finally waived this requirement in view of the gravity of the matter:

> This case is one of the most important which has been presented to your Courts. The murder was a brutal, barbarous assassination. . . . It has attracted the attention of the whole country. It has been alluded to in debate in the Congress of the nation.[30]

But Cunningham was not yet in the courtroom. Delivered to Creek authorities, he made his escape back to the Cherokee Nation, and the extradition process had to be repeated. It was prolonged when a new Cherokee chief took over and some of the legal steps had to be retraced. Finally returned to Creek custody, he managed to escape again and, as public interest in the case waned, Cunningham faded into obscurity, a free man.

The murder of the Cherokee policeman did focus attention on the need for a change in the law. Not until 1965 did it become a federal offense to kill a President of the United States, but Indian policemen have been protected for years under an act which is testimony to the stature of Captain Samuel Sixkiller and may be considered his memorial. An appropriation act passed in March 1887 carried a section extending the protection of federal law to the Indian

30. Parker to Perryman, May 3, 1887 (Creek Foreign Relations File).

police, and it was replaced by a more definitive legislation in June 1888.

While legislators debated ways to protect them, being an Indian policeman continued to be a risky business. Sixkiller's successor as captain of Union Agency police lasted only three months before he was shot to death. Indian juries in the Union Agency seemed to reflect a bias against policemen. A lieutenant on the force killed a thug in self-defense and was convicted of manslaughter. In another case Chickasaw jurors condemned an Indian member of a posse as an accessory in the killing of a tribesman, while a federal court freed a white man who was the principal in the case. As their agent once remarked: "They do their work, not for the small salary, but in a public spirit, *pro bono publico.*"[31]

31. Owen to CIA (n. 23 above).

4. Agents of the Civilization Process

ALTHOUGH the necessity for coping with renegades and common criminal elements was the original reason for organizing the Indian police, another use to which they would be put appeared in an early draft to the appropriation bill authorizing them. It provided that they should be employed also "for the purposes of civilization of the Indians,"[1] which eventually was to inspire some of the most interesting, if debatable, duties of the Indian police.

Some reformers in the late nineteenth century criticized the use of force in civilizing the Indians. They supported the policy of converting the Indians into peace-loving Christians making their living by farming until they were ready for the next move up the ladder of cultural evolution. In this the Indian police would lead the way by enforcing the edicts of the Indian Office and, as Commissioner of Indian Affairs E. M. Marble once phrased it, bring "into an agency a new element . . . which grasps the idea of the supremacy of law, and which by precept and example inculcates that idea." Commissioner Marble also referred to the offenses "many of which hitherto have not only gone unpunished, but have been unrecognized as meriting punishment," manifesting the popular view that Indian cultures were incapable of developing rational and effective systems of social control.[2]

As Marble's "precept and example," the policeman had

1. *Congressional Record*, 7 (4) (1878), 3770.
2. AR of Marble, 1880 (ser. 1959, p. 88).

his work cut out for him. He must cleave to one wife, and his appearance should reflect his commitment to the civilization program. Accordingly, the policeman was supposed to give up his long braids, cease painting his face, trade moccasins for boots, and eschew any other outward manifestation of the blanket Indian. But that was the easiest part of it. The policeman also had to see that work assignments were carried out, prohibit deeply entrenched activities like dancing, gambling, and raiding for horses, oppose the influence of medicine men and witches, enforce school attendance, and support the agent and the Progressives against the Conservatives.

On some reservations the ban on long braids violated not only Indian aesthetics but, infinitely more important, their religious concepts. Even the more acculturated Indians, as for example a woman who had served as an interpreter at the Bannock–Shoshone Agency, could believe that burning a child's hair after cutting it would cause his death.[3] Agents, nevertheless, insisted that their policemen crop their own hair, and occasionally police had to try to enforce the edict for all reservation males. Most policemen conformed to the order to cut their hair or get off the force, but a chief of police and a private from the Mescalero Apache force quit over the issue. Their agent possibly stopped a general police strike over haircuts by threatening to stop rations to the remainder of the force if they joined the dissenters. What makes the police obstinacy on the braid issue even more impressive is that they accepted an order to force hats, coats, vests, shirts, pants, and shoes on every male Mescalero who had attended school! This agent would tolerate no backsliding among returned students.[4]

If as an all-reservation policy it caused too much friction,

3. AR of S. G. Fisher, 1892 (ser. 3088, p. 233).
4. AR of V. E. Stottler, 1896 (ser. 3489, p. 211).

the ban on braids was usually quietly dropped. Hoot-et-soot, of the Umatilla Reservation, was awarded $25 in damages by an Oregon state court when he sued after being forcibly barbered in jail.[5] Such legal actions tended to discourage overzealous agents, who soon discovered they could not depend on backing from Washington if they ran afoul of state or territorial courts in implementing the civilization program.

No such legal problem arose in giving preference for police positions to those Indians who had taken up allotments, after the Dawes Severalty Act had enshrined that policy. But it was difficult to get Indians who were conscientious about their farming, and thus setting the best example, who could spare time for a policeman's duties. One Sioux agent's solution was to cut duty assignments in half during the busiest farm months and hope the criminal element would cooperate by observing a summer schedule.[6]

Even a part-time schedule could be burdensome for an Indian. As an advance agent of the white man's way he frequently found himself opposed by most of his fellow tribesmen, especially the old, respected leaders. Cast as an informer, a petty police spy, he had to report on the work habits of bands to determine whether they merited sugar, coffee, tobacco, and other rations. Such a role would be difficult in any society.

In trying to impose the value judgments of one culture on another, the white administrators assigned some unusual tasks to the police. One captain of police wrote up wills for dying Indians because that agent was particularly disturbed by the tribal practice of giving away the movable property of the deceased and then destroying his house.[7]

5. CIA to Sec. of the Interior, Feb. 14, 1896 (OIALR, 5441, 1896).
6. AR of E. W. Foster, 1891 (ser. 2934, p. 428).
7. J. B. McLane to CIA, July 28, 1888 (OIALR, 19654, 1888).

The efficiency of the police normally declined as the intimacy of such duties intensified. One official after another reported that his police were reluctant to arrest their friends and relatives, these ties being particularly strong in Indian societies. They were on occasion, however, drawn into domestic crises. The Assinaboine force was appealed to when Raider, a young man of the tribe, beat his wife. Big Mouth, her brother, brought in the police, for which the indignant Raider killed him. Raider's father, Lodge-in-Timber, came to his support and the two of them defied the agent and wounded the white man in the leg. The father and son then fled the Fort Belknap Agency and headed for Canada. On the open prairie, loyal Assinaboine police caught them and, despite bullets through a coat and a hat of the pursuers, brought them down.[8]

Shooting an agent was obviously criminal, but horse theft was an intertribal affair that was difficult to get the police to take seriously. Among the Blackfeet such actions were regarded as "retaliation" or "justice."[9] The size of one's pony herd was a matter of status, and skill in adding to it Crow or Sioux horses had always been a highly admired competence of the Blackfeet.

Gambling was another favorite Indian pastime the police had to be taught to recognize as a crime. A Kiowa–Comanche agent observed ruefully that on his reservation his force included some of the "most expert" gamblers.[10]

Coping with medicine men and witches was beyond the capacity of the average force, since it required a denial of supernatural influences which were an integral part of their cultural heritage. Captain Black Coyote, Cheyenne veteran

8. A. O. Simmons to CIA, Dec. 12, 1892 (OIALR, 44811, 1892); Dec. 13, 1892 (OIALR, 44812, 1892).

9. AR of John Young, 1882 (ser. 2100, p. 159).

10. AR of J. Lee Hall, 1886 (ser. 2467, p. 348).

of eighteen years on the force, had been entrusted with such delicate assignments as a mission to the Shoshone country to investigate the myth of the Messiah, the religious cult that was Sitting Bull's downfall. Nevertheless, Black Coyote still clung to some of the old beliefs: he summoned tribal medicine men to treat two of his children who were ill and refused offers of aid from the agency physician. The children died, and the exasperated agent removed the veteran from the force.[11]

In a comparable situation Nannice, a member of the Ute police, availed himself of the aid of both medicine men and the agency physician when his child fell ill. Then when the medicine men quarreled among themselves, Nannice stabbed one of them to death and forfeited his badge.[12]

Apache neighbors of the Utes presented the same problem. Their force was described as always reliable except when they had been ordered to capture the Indians "who shot the woman accused of being a witch."[13] Nearly a thousand miles away in Oregon the agent of a reservation that housed remnants of several tribes also had medicine-man trouble. All of his Indians who were questioned testified to a belief in the power of shamans over life and death. Car-polis, a policeman who had served the United States faithfully in the Modoc War, replied that he would arrest a medicine man if so ordered, although it would surely cost him his life.[14] Most policemen were not so dedicated to duty as Car-polis, and on reservations where these beliefs persisted, the police generally were unable to transcend their religious backgrounds. Here and there the agency physicians gained a convert, although it might not be an easy process.

11. AR of A. E. Woodson, 1896 (ser. 3489, p. 249).
12. Charles Bartholomew to CIA, April 2, 1891 (Southern Ute LB).
13. AR of Wm. H. H. Llewellyn, 1885 (ser. 2379, p. 377).
14. AR of Jason Wheeler, 1886 (ser. 2467, p. 441).

A member of a Mohave force, on the advice of tribal elders, threw away medicine prescribed for his child by the white physician. When the child died the policeman was removed from the force, and he subsequently acknowledged his mistake.[15]

Parental devotion was a factor in complicating another police chore—keeping the Indian schools full. Education was one of the great panaceas offered for tribal primitivism. Reformers might argue the relative merits of day schools, reservation boarding schools, and Captain Pratt's institution at Carlisle, but they agreed on the absolute necessity that each Indian child be exposed to the ABCs and school discipline. Some went so far as to advocate that the Indian pupil be denied vacation visits home, on the theory that he would regress. Where such policies prevailed, a child might not see his family for two or three years. Very few Indian parents detected any merit in this system, for deep parental love and kindness characterized all tribal cultures, whatever might have been their other differences. And the high mortality rate among students at government schools, as the strange climates and diseases took their toll, certainly would have discouraged any parent, white or red, from entrusting his child to them. Ironically, a white agent's concern for his own daughter's teaching career at Haskell Institute led him to ignore such fears among his charges. This agent was charged with transferring Indian children to Haskell, without consulting their parents, in order to enhance his own daughter's position there.[16]

When called upon to round up students for the schools, when other tactics such as curtailing rations or cutting off annuity payments had failed, some policemen flatly refused. Shoshone and Bannock police quit en masse on one such

15. AR of Charles F. Ashley, 1886 (ser. 2467, p. 253).
16. Edw. L. Thomas to CIA, April 5, 1894 (Sac and Fox LB).

occasion.[17] Several years later on the same reservation they did enforce the agent's edict that a fourteen-year-old bride attend school. Her husband took exception and, when the agent refused to release his bride, the bereft mate and his friends kidnapped her from the school. Getting into the spirit of the thing, other young men raided the school and released all the young girls, claiming they also were wives. The Indian youths beat up the police who interfered, and it took cavalry to restore order.[18]

The fear and hysteria the police inspired in the role of truant officers are chillingly illustrated in two accounts, one contemporary, the other an impressionistic reconstruction by a modern writer of Osage ancestry. The contemporary account by a Mescalero Apache agent related to his efforts to stock the local boarding school:

> Everything in the way of persuasion and argument having failed, it became necessary to visit the camps unexpectedly with a detachment of police, and seize such children as were proper. . . . Some hurried their children off to the mountains or hid them away in camp, and the police had to chase and capture them like so many wild rabbits. The men were sullen and muttering, the women loud in their lamentations, and the children almost out of their wits with fright.[19]

The Osage reconstruction supplies the sordid details the official report only suggests. Yet J. J. Mathews' account of police tactics is probably little exaggerated, although it may come as a shock to generations oriented toward student participation and teacher–student planning:

17. Brigham D. Madsen, *The Bannock of Idaho* (Caldwell, 1958), p. 313.
18. Ibid., p. 324.
19. AR of Fletcher J. Cowart, 1886 (ser. 2467, p. 417).

when the girls resisted, [the police] would hold their
arms behind their backs and load them in the wagon,
tying them to the bow slots. When after reaching the
agency some of them jumped from the wagons and ran,
the police overtook them on their horses, and roping
them, they would drag them up the dusty hill to the
school buildings.

These were the older girls, who fought like brought-
to-bay bobcats. They would fall as they struggled
against the ropes, and their long black hair would
make traces in the deep dust of the road, and their
clothing was rent, but unlike the brought-to-bay bob-
cat, they would make no sounds and there were no
tears; only silence and sweat that muddied the dust of
their faces.[20]

Inevitably these tactics inspired violence among those
resisting the education program. A captain of police was
almost killed when he seized a twelve-year-old Apache–
Mohave truant when the boy ventured too near the agency.
The boy's father had the largest herds in the tribe and was
a Progressive on many issues but adamant in refusing to
enroll his ample brood of children in the agency school.
Shortly after the boy had been picked up, an older brother
arrived on horseback at the school grounds, mounted the
boy behind him, and started for home. The captain and
another policeman overtook them and recaptured the boy.
Before they could reach the school the brother, now accompanied by his father, reappeared. In the fight that followed, the
father broke his knife off in one policeman's arm, and his
older son drove his blade into the captain's back, penetrating
a lung. As the captain fell he managed to reach his revolver

20. John Joseph Mathews, *The Osages* (Norman, 1961), p. 730.

and to wound the father in the leg, but the boy was once again free.[21]

Similar difficulties at the Navajo reservation in the 1890s almost precipitated a major uprising. In pursuance of orders to fill the local school, Agent David L. Shipley turned his attention to a portion of the reservation which had supplied no pupils. Accompanied by three other whites and seven members of his police force, Shipley counseled at Round Rock with Black Horse, a leader of the Navajos opposing all innovations. Black Horse not only refused to provide any pupils, he demanded that the children of Progressive bands be sent home. Harangued by Black Horse, other Navajos rushed the agent, pummeling him thoroughly and breaking his nose. They might have killed him if his companions had not intervened, one of the policemen getting a bad wound in the process. Aided by a friendly Indian who helped clear the way, the agent's party was able to retreat to a store building and barricade it. With only two rifles, two pistols, and fifty rounds of ammunition to hold off the excited Navajos, the besieged were in a tight spot. Black Horse's followers stayed in the vicinity for thirty-six hours, shouting insults at the agent, who reported in stilted prose that their "crazed and defiant yells . . . had a tendency to place a very unsatisfactory and alarming phaze to our situation." A timely downpour assuaged the fears of the besieged that the Navajos might burn them out. Their ordeal was finally ended by the arrival of a small detachment of cavalry, alerted by a policeman who in the confusion had managed to slip away.[22]

More than the school policy had alienated Black Horse, and he was typical of the Conservatives who disliked the general trend of the civilization program. Sometimes it was

21. Charles S. McNichols to CIA, May 2, 1898 (OIALR, 22367, 1898).

22. David L. Shipley to CIA, Nov. 2, 1892 (OIALR, 40407, 1892).

not a case of the Conservatives' adherence to their aboriginal
culture but simply a matter of vital statistics and parental
devotion. Of twenty-four Southern Ute children recruited
for an Albuquerque school, twelve died while they were
students or suspiciously soon after they returned to their
families.[23] The hostility of Ute parents to any school program was a logical result. Ignacio, Captain of Indian Police
and Principal Chief of his people, and a Progressive on other
issues, led the opposition to sending Ute children to a new
boarding school in Fort Lewis, Oregon. For this stand, despite Ignacio's services, which had led the Indian Office to
support his claims to chieftainship and his agent to designate
him as "One of, if not, the Best Indians in the Tribe,"
Ignacio lost his captain's commission.[24]

Although a proposed resettlement of the tribe was a
possible factor in his stand, the Ute defended himself by
referring solely to the tragic experience of their children with
schools and the illness already plaguing the Fort Lewis institution. Caught between frightened Ute parents and an
impersonal bureaucracy in Washington demanding compliance with directives, the agent tried bribery. At least two
Indians were promised positions on the police force if they
would send their children to school. By such means sixteen
Ute children were shipped off to Fort Lewis. Within a year
two were dead and three others, including one whose father
was bribed by promise of a job, were totally blind, presumably victims of a disease contracted at the school.[25] It is
little wonder that recruiting pupils was so distasteful to the
policemen themselves.

Ignacio represented a type of Indian whom the whites
had helped elevate to tribal leadership. Able men in their

23. H. B. Freeman to CIA, Aug. 24, 1893 (Southern Ute LB).
24. List of Southern Utes, June 31, 1890, ibid.
25. H. B. Freeman to CIA, Aug. 24, 1893; Dec. 12, 1893, ibid.

own right, the Ignacios were willing to be used as front men for agency officials. Some may have sold out, others may have concluded that the changes they were being asked to advance were inevitable or needed or both. As chiefs and headmen they might serve as police themselves, or they might recommend men who could command respect and then back them. White officials learned to prize the Ignacios, and the agent ordered to depose the Ute chief for his school stand vigorously protested Ignacio's value to the efficient administration of the reservation.

While agents might find it convenient to work through the traditional tribal structure to achieve a smoothly running reservation, those concerned with the larger aspects of Indian policy had concluded that the time had come to uproot the tribe as an institution. In his 1881 annual report, Commissioner of Indian Affairs Hiram Price commented that the police system was "a power entirely independent of the chiefs. It weakens, and will finally destroy, the power of tribes and bands."[26] His confidence may have been inspired by reports he had just read from the Oto and Western Shoshone agencies. From the Oto Agency came word that the chiefs were "rather jealous" of the police, over whom they had no control. The Oto agent judged the police experiment "an excellent scheme, as it has a tendency to break up tribal relations and reduce the power of the chiefs." He reported with obvious satisfaction that he was "importuned almost daily by the chiefs to appoint men that I know to be under their control. . . . As it is, the Police are a check upon the chiefs, and they report any thing that transpires in the tribe."[27]

At the Western Shoshone Agency also, the police were credited with helping disrupt tribal relations. Captain Sam,

26. AR of Price, 1881 (ser. 2018, p. 13).
27. Lewellyn E. Woodin to CIA, Sept. 6, 1881 (Oto LB).

the Principal Chief, was no more successful than his Oto counterparts in preventing Indians from taking police positions. Yet these were only two of forty-nine agencies with forces in 1881, and each was a unique situation. The determining factor in one might be the length of time the Indians had been exposed to reservation atmosphere; in another it would be the personalities of the antagonists. Where a chief of the stature and competence of the Nez Percé Joseph, or the Shoshone Washakie, declined to cooperate, recruiting police could be impossible. Washakie was generally considered a Progressive, but against the police he used a simple argument: "Shoshones are not white people."[28]

On those reservations where the Indians had been pacified only recently, there was always the problem of what were dubbed "renegades" or "hostiles." In the summer of 1882 the Mescalero force emerged from such a situation with mixed honors. Their time of trial came when a few renegades slipped into the reservation with some stolen stock and joined the camp of Give-Me-a-Horse. This Mescalero was himself an escaped prisoner, having eluded the military at Fort Union. When the agent learned of their presence, he collected a force of police and white personnel and surprised the renegades' camp. The hostiles refused to surrender, and two of them and their host were killed, the others escaping to the mountains in a running fight. The agent was hit twice in the left arm, but possibly more disturbing to him was the desertion of one of his police in the heat of battle. The Mescalero chief of police attributed the desertion to the defector's having a brother among the renegades slain. Once again family ties had triumphed.[29]

28. AR of James I. Patten, 1879 (ser. 1910, p. 274).
29. Wm. H. H. Llewellyn to CIA, June 23, 1882; June 24, 1882 (Mescalero LB); James L. Smith to Llewellyn, July 1, 1882, ibid.; AR of Llewellyn, 1882 (ser. 2100, pp. 185–86).

Troubles of this nature, unwelcome as they may have been, could not have surprised an agent, but that Apaches, of all Indians, should plead pacifism as an excuse for leaving their police force was unexpected. Since the practice of using Indians to trail renegade bands had been emphasized by General Crook, it had been common practice for police from the various Apache tribes to be detailed to such temporary duty. Thus the consternation at agency headquarters can be imagined when the entire force of Jicarilla Apaches resigned in anticipation of being employed against renegades from another clan. With provokingly sound logic they pled "that instead of war like pursuits that it is peaceful pursuits they desire."[30]

Once again it had been demonstrated that Indian reaction to alien institutions forced upon them could not be predicted with any degree of accuracy. Nevertheless, Indian police were invaluable in helping supervise the transition of a nomadic warrior people to a more peaceful, sedentary way of life. This was nowhere better demonstrated than on the Great Sioux Reserve.

30. James H. Roberts to B. M. Thomas, May 16, 1879 (Albiquiu LB).

5. A Sioux Sampler

IN THE FALL OF 1878 all the Sioux tribes, which had supplied most of the hostiles in the Sioux War of 1876, were settled on the Great Sioux Reserve, covering over half of present-day South Dakota. Originally six agencies comprised the huge reservation: Cheyenne River, Pine Ridge, Rosebud, Standing Rock, Crow Creek, and Lower Brulé, but the last two were consolidated in 1882. All the problems encountered at other agencies seemed to be compounded here. There were more Indians, more room for them to roam, more opposition to the civilization programs, and, along the Nebraska line and at the landings on the Missouri River, more whites to interfere. The problem of agent tenure was about the same. In the twelve years from the organization of the first police forces through their severest test, the Ghost Dance, three of the agencies had had at least five different administrative heads, one had three, and the other two. And this was the type of job a man did not learn in a few months.

The Cheyenne River Agency was one of the least populous and least troublesome, which was fortunate since it had five administrative changes in this period. Its Indian population was drawn from several Sioux tribes, but only one, the Miniconjou, had been involved with Sitting Bull. In the spring of 1878 a new agent came to these Indians from Fort Pierre, the garrison on the reservation. There is no evidence that the "Acting Agent," as Captain Theodore

Schwan always signed himself, sought the assignment. Five months after being detailed as agent he sought permission to return to "legitimate duties with my Co. [of the 11th Infantry]."[1] Two years were to pass, however, before he would be back with troops. In the interim, Captain Schwan organized the first police force at his agency and brought some order into an administration which had suffered under his last two predecessors, both of whom had been dismissed for poor performance.

The new agent was a native of Germany, a no-nonsense administrator and a career officer who had earned his commission and a Congressional Medal of Honor during the Civil War. Captain Schwan recognized immediately the potential of police in providing agents with the "physical power to enforce obedience and to punish refractory and criminal Indians." Some saw a Prussian background in such a dictum as: "The Indian respects and readily yields to physical force, but is sometimes hard to move by arguments, however cogent, or advice, however well meant."[2] These views, which could have been held by almost any of his fellow officers, Prussian-born or not, helped earn him the Indian nickname, The-Man-Who-Never-Smiles.[3]

Although Schwan received orders in June 1878 to recruit a police force at Cheyenne River, he did not accomplish it until the following November, citing inadequate pay and the lack of weapons and uniforms for the delay. Once it was organized, the captain lavished on the force the attention he would have preferred to give his infantry company. The police were drilled in the manual of arms, and every Monday Schwan would have them paraded for his weekly inspections which, he declared like the infantry officer he

1. Schwan to CIA, Aug. 21, 1878 (OIALR, Roll 130).
2. AR of Schwan, 1879 (ser. 1910, p. 129).
3. George E. Hyde, *A Sioux Chronicle* (Norman, 1956), p. 30.

was, "are absolutely essential to the efficiency and discipline of the force."[4]

From an original nine men, Cheyenne River's force had expanded to twenty by July 1879. With this "more potent stimulus than moral suasion,"[5] Captain Schwan moved energetically to discourage his charges from engaging in the "cruel" and barbarous" Sun Dance. This ceremony featured warriors bearing buffalo skulls, dancing around an upright pole or being suspended from one. The skulls were tied to the Indian, or the Indian to the pole, by slits in the skin of his upper trunk. To achieve the full benefit of the ceremony, in the course of his dance the participant had to tear his skin to free himself.

Although he was able to ban the Sun Dance from Cheyenne River, Schwan found it very difficult to prevent his Indians from accepting invitations from their friends and neighbors at Rosebud Agency to join them there for the celebrations. The agent who was Schwan's contemporary at Rosebud managed his Indians with a very lax hand, and the captain complained that his own Indians, as a result, considered themselves persecuted. He also attributed some of his problems to the lack of clearly defined agency boundaries.[6] In 1879 the six Sioux agencies still constituted, from the Indian viewpoint, one great Sioux reservation over which they had the right to wander at will.

A report compiled for the second quarter of 1879 by the chief of police for the Cheyenne River force indicated that keeping Schwan's charges at home, and uninvited Indian guests away, constituted much of the police duty. One entry reveals that Private George No Heart arrested Little Elk, a Rosebud Indian, on charges that he had entered the reserva-

4. Schwan to CIA, April 1, 1879 (OIALR, Roll 131).
5. Schwan (n. 2 above).
6. Schwan to CIA, Oct. 10, 1879; Oct. 21, 1879 (OIALR, Roll 131).

tion without permission and was encouraging Cheyenne River Indians to slip over to Rosebud. Little Elk was placed in a cell for twenty-four hours to discourage him from such conduct in the future. Other entries recorded that Privates White Buffalo Man, Galloper, Crane, and Slow Eagle called at the Indian camps to discourage visits to the Rosebud Sun Dance and locked up Red Feather overnight for having attended the dance. The police also investigated the report of an attempted rape, arrested a thief and returned some calico he had stolen, and checked a report of whites cutting timber from the reservation's slender resources. Additional routine duties for the police were carrying messages and being stationed at the office, shops, and warehouses on issue days to keep order and to help where needed.[7]

When Schwan finally was preparing to return to his beloved infantry company, he wrote a long letter to the Indian Commissioner embodying his views on reservation administration. He described the Cheyenne River police force as "on the whole, in a satisfactory condition," but complained of the salaries paid them. The captain recommended that a higher rate of pay for nine, or even six police, would be preferable to an eighteen-man force whose salaries were so low as "to expose them to the ridicule of other Indians."[8] Whether a force of six or eighteen, it was obvious that he had a high opinion of the innovation made during his tenure as agent. Schwan's successors at Cheyenne River also recognized the police as a valuable instrument. The agents' only complaints were that they could not have as many police as they would like and could not pay them as much as they deserved.

Appointment to the police was tried as a means to woo Conservatives into the Progressive camp. Hump, a Minicon-

7. Record of Cheyenne River Police, April–June 1879, ibid.
8. Schwan to CIA, July 26, 1880, ibid.

jou, was made chief of police in the hope that the distinction
would win him over, but the strategy failed. His camp on
Cherry Creek continued to be a center of Conservative opposition to government programs. In the late 1880s pressure
was brought to bear on the Sioux to accept allotment and
sell their surplus land, but Hump, complete with badge and
uniform, was in the forefront of the dissenters.[9]

Straddling the Missouri River some distance below
Hump's preserve was the Crow Creek and Lower Brulé
Consolidated Agency. Most of the excitement there was
provided by the Teton tribe, the Lower Brulés. They occupied the west bank of the Missouri and enjoyed a fiercer
reputation than the Yanktonais of Crow Creek. The intran-
sigence of the Lower Brulés was heightened by contact with
their relatives, the Brulés of Spotted Tail's band, on the
Rosebud Reservation to the southwest. Only a few months
after their organization, the Lower Brulé police were totally
demoralized by an assault upon them by a hundred young
warriors, inflamed by the speeches of White Thunder, one
of Spotted Tail's headmen. Stripped for war, they dashed
through the camps threatening to kill any Indian volunteer-
ing for the police. Seeking out Bull Head and Omaha, who
had agreed to join the force, the mob broke windows in their
cabins and killed their chickens, pigs, and dogs. When Bull
Head and Omaha were finally cornered, pistols and rifles
were held on them until they agreed to get off the force. The
other police were then rounded up and similarly threatened;
Indians otherwise employed at the agency were also intimidated.[10]

The Lower Brulé chiefs had not taken a leading role in

9. Harry H. Anderson, "A History of the Cheyenne River Indian
Agency and Its Military Post, Fort Bennett," M.A. Thesis (1954), p. 146.
10. William G. Dougherty to CIA, March 24, 1879 (OIALR, Roll
268).

the demonstration, but behind the scenes they had encouraged it. Called before the agent for a lecture, Dead Hand argued that the Indians at Rosebud were not watched by police, and the Lower Brulés were being imposed upon. In the same vein, Medicine Bull said that by tribal custom "their grandfathers" policed the band and there was no need for a police force. He disparaged the excitement over breaking a few windows and doors and pointed out that neither that property, nor the livestock killed, had belonged to whites.[11] Such arguments did not mollify the agent, and he considered calling in troops but settled for withdrawing sugar and coffee rations from the troublemakers. Subsequently he reorganized the force, but he testified it was "not efficient or reliable, and cannot be so when every man is equally well armed and reserves the right to be his own policeman."[12]

At the Rosebud Agency the police were even less dependable. Until his death in 1881 the agency was dominated by the Brulé chief Spotted Tail. A noted warrior in his youth, he had surrendered to the whites for his part in the destruction of a small detachment of troops under Lieutenant Grattan. Released after two years' imprisonment Spotted Tail aligned himself with those Sioux who had accepted the futility of further resistance by armed force. Still, he did not become a supine tool of the Indian Bureau—Spotted Tail would cooperate, but on his terms. He tolerated a police force at Rosebud only so long as he approved the selections for the force.

Agent Cicero Newell once came up with a plan to free the force from the influence of "Spot," as he called the Sioux chief. The agent proposed to disband the old force: "The only duty they have ever been known to perform, was

11. Dougherty to CIA, March 28, ibid.
12. AR of Dougherty, 1880 (ser. 1959, p. 160).

drawing their pay, which they did with the utmost regularity."[13] Their replacements would then be carried on the agency payroll as night herders, extra laborers, and ox teamsters, thus receiving salaries of $30 to $50 a month. But, despite Newell's having conferred with Secretary of Interior Schurz on the matter, this scheme was vetoed by the Commissioner of Indian Affairs, who pointed out that the salary of police was set by law.[14]

A few months later in a communication to Washington, Spotted Tail made clear the position he had carved out for himself: "My agent and I act together. I am chief of all this people and he is the agent sent to help me, by the 'Great Father.' "[15] The agent Spotted Tail was referring to was a new man, John Cook, but he had more backbone than Cicero Newell. The Brulé chief soon challenged Cook's control of the police force, and lost. The confrontation developed from a difference between the agency traders and Spotted Tail. To bring them into line the chief stationed police to bar any Indian customers from the traders' stores. Cook learned of the picketing, hastened to the scene, and ordered the police to return to duty. With one exception they refused, pleading their first allegiance to Chief Spotted Tail. After a stormy session with the chief and a meeting of the tribal council, Agent Cook emerged the clear victor.[16]

A few weeks later he had occasion to be proud of his police. Five young Brulé warriors had followed Turning Bear on a horse raid into Nebraska. Returning to the reservation with seven prizes and the scalp of a white man, their boasts brought them to the attention of Spotted Tail who,

13. Newell to CIA, Oct. 15, 1879 (OIALR, Roll 844).
14. Schurz to CIA, Sept. 4, 1879 (OIALR, Roll 724); Newell to CIA, Sept. 4, 1879 (OIALR, Roll 844).
15. Spotted Tail to the President, Aug. 4, 1880 (OIALR, Roll 845).
16. AR of Cook, 1880 (ser. 1959, pp. 168–69).

now in his role of Progressive, reported them to Cook. The agent directed Captain Crow Dog of the Indian police to take the raiders into custody and deliver them to Fort Randall, 135 miles away. Accompanied by a lone white man, Crow Dog and a detachment of eighteen police delivered the prisoners and stolen horses to the commanding officer at the post. To impress the Sioux, Colonel George L. Andrews outfitted Crow Dog with a colonel's uniform coat and paraded his "black soldiers" before the Brulés.[17] Flattered by the attention, the Indian captain returned to Rosebud where he subsequently became associated with a faction opposing Spotted Tail in an intratribal power struggle. It culminated in a fatal encounter after a Brulé council. At point-blank range Crow Dog suddenly leveled a rifle at Spotted Tail and shot him through the left breast. The chief died, struggling to draw his revolver; Crow Dog, who had previously left the force, was taken into custody by Eagle Hawk, the new captain of police.[18] Efforts to bring Crow Dog to justice had repercussions affecting the entire system for maintaining law and order on Indian reservations.

Rosebud had resisted the innovation, and Pine Ridge and Standing Rock agencies were equally tough testing grounds for the concept of an Indian police. At Pine Ridge the order to organize the police arrived at an awkward time. Agent James Irwin, defeated by the problems he encountered, was in the process of resigning. The Sioux, he had concluded, "will never be cured of their *importance,* and *arrogance,* and *willful stubbornness,* until they are made to feel the power of the government."[19] And Irwin specified how this should be accomplished—by General Crook's troopers. The retiring

17. Ibid.; Cook to CIA, Aug. 9, and Aug. 16, 1880 (OIALR, Roll 845).
18. AR of Cook, 1881 (ser. 2018, p. 112).
19. Irwin to CIA, Feb. 20, 1878 (OIALR, Roll 722).

agent also felt that he had not received the cooperation of the Indian Office, and of Commissioner E. A. Hayt specifically.

Irwin's replacement was Dr. V. T. McGillycuddy, a strong-willed army surgeon with considerable Plains experience. An Indian Inspector recommended him as being "a constructing organizing man" and one with "plenty of backing and friends," a real necessity in the unpleasent infighting that characterized relations among agents, contractors, settlers, local politicians, and the Indian Office.[20]

When the doctor took over on March 1, 1879, the first tentative moves had been made to raise the police force. Here, as elsewhere, a big stumbling block was the poor pay. McGillycuddy contrasted the $5 per month salary of the police with the $24 he said an army scout could draw in pay and allowances.[21] He also mentioned other opposition, which Secretary Schurz spelled out while touring the Great Sioux Reserve. The chiefs were throwing their influence against the police, but Schurz thought that some lectures by himself had brought them around. As a solution to the pay problem the Secretary made the same proposal he had discussed with Newell at Rosebud: classify the police as laborers until Congress granted raises. He also came up with an interesting way out of the equipment shortage; he suggested treating the police like militia companies and drawing their arms and accouterments from the War Department.[22] Neither of these ingenious, but slightly dubious, solutions was acceptable to more legalistic administrators.

One reason for authorizing as large a force as fifty men for Pine Ridge was that Nebraska lay along its southern boundary. Just over the state line was a large Mexican settle-

20. J. H. Hammond to CIA, Nov. 23, ibid.
21. McGillycuddy to CIA, Aug. 4, 1879 (OIALR, Roll 724).
22. Schurz to CIA, Sept. 4, 1879, ibid.

ment which McGillycuddy believed to be a "rendezvous for criminals and outlaws of all kinds."[23] Besides helping keep the reservation free of such undesirable elements, he hoped the police would furnish leverage against Red Cloud, the principal chief at Rosebud.

This famous Oglala had led Sioux warriors in their successful effort to close the Bozeman Trail in the 1860s. In many ways the proud veteran of the Wagon Box Fight and the Fetterman Massacre resembled Spotted Tail. McGillycuddy saw the similarity, referring to the two elderly Sioux chiefs as "about as egregious a pair of old frauds . . . as it has ever been my fortune or misfortune to encounter."[24] The former army surgeon had no sympathy for the tribal Conservatives and their white allies, and he once evicted from his agency T. A. Bland, editor of *Council Fire* and a critic of civilization policies. McGillycuddy's own views were rather commonplace among military personnel in the late nineteenth century: "The Indian is brutal in many ways and low in the evolutionary scale as a human being." The agent was willing to grant only that the Indian was "endowed with reasoning power, and a conscience to a certain degree."[25]

Unless he proposed to let Red Cloud and his backers run the reservation, McGillycuddy's fifty-man force was absolutely indispensable in administering the 4,000 square miles inhabited by 8,000 Indians. And after 1881 his responsibilities included about 600 of Sitting Bull's former hostiles. Another band giving the doctor some worried moments was composed of Northern Cheyennes headed by Little Chief and Wild Hog, followers of Red Cloud in reservation matters.

23. McGillycuddy to CIA (n. 21 above).
24. AR of McGillycuddy, 1880 (ser. 1959, p. 162).
25. AR of McGillycuddy, 1881 (ser. 2018, p. 103).

McGillycuddy's disenchantment with Red Cloud was a gradual process extending over about a year and a half. Eight months after the doctor took over the agency he could request government aid in furnishing Red Cloud's new government-built four-room cottage, and justify it in terms of the old chief's "using every endeavor for the good of the agency and his tribe."[26] As late as March 1880 McGillycuddy wanted to buy a light spring wagon and team for Red Cloud who, he said, was "behaving himself in an exemplary manner."[27] But the chief had apparently used his influence against the recruitment of a police force, and in the summer of 1880 he allowed himself to become identified with a few squaw men, traders, and mixed-bloods disputing agency affairs with McGillycuddy. The final rupture between the agent and Red Cloud was caused by a letter critical of the doctor and signed by Red Cloud, but presumably written by a trader belonging to the anti-McGillycuddy faction. The agent's enemies had written another letter and persuaded American Horse, a minor chief, to place his X on it. In both cases McGillycuddy regarded the chiefs as just the facade behind which the whites and mixed-bloods operated. Red Cloud, he observed, "is now an old man in his dotage, childish and not responsible for what he does."[28]

To oppose Red Cloud, Dr. McGillycuddy had built up the Progressive chief Young-Man-Afraid-of-His-Horses, who in turn suggested appointing Man-Who-Carries-the-Sword (George Sword) as captain of police.[29] A Progressive, yet a young warrior respected in the tribe for his feats in raiding enemy horse herds, Captain Sword proved as loyal a subordinate as any agent could hope to have.

26. McGillycuddy to CIA, Dec. 2, 1879 (OIALR, Roll 725).
27. McGillycuddy to CIA, March 16, 1880 (OIALR, Roll 726).
28. McGillycuddy to CIA, Nov. 15, ibid.
29. Julia B. McGillycuddy, *McGillycuddy: Agent* (Stanford, 1941), p. 113.

Transforming the fifty young recruits into a competent force was slowed by the usual delay of the Indian Office in supplying them with rifles. McGillycuddy was able to exploit his army contacts to borrow fifty carbines from the ordnance stores at Fort Robinson, but not until October 1880 did the Indian Office ship him arms, allowing him to return those he had borrowed.[30] The doctor also acquired the services of an old cavalry first sergeant who trained the Pine Ridge police to perform mounted drills, to McGillycuddy's obvious delight. The first evidence that the doctor was fashioning a potent weapon as well as a parade-ground ornament was its handling of Spotted Wolf, in a situation resembling the Turning Bear affair at Rosebud.

Spotted Wolf, a Northern Cheyenne, was an agency troublemaker reputed to have lifted the scalps of three Kansas settlers. His final escapade was to elope with the daughter of the famous Cheyenne chief Dull Knife. The lovers were accompanied by three other warriors, five women, and a child. To speed their flight they relieved the band of Young-Man-Afraid-of-His-Horses of twenty-two of their mounts. Advised of their escape, McGillycuddy ordered Captain Sword and nine men in hot pursuit. The renegades had a twelve-hour start and were not overtaken until they were west of the Black Hills, about 125 miles from the agency. Surrounded while encamped, Spotted Wolf refused to surrender. Throwing off his blanket in a gesture of defiance, the Cheyenne warrior indicated his readiness to fight. He paid for his temerity with his life, and Sword delivered his corpse on a travois to the agency office, to the accompaniment of the keening of Cheyenne women. The captain received the warm congratulations of his agent, but his fellow tribesmen fined him fifteen ponies for taking another Indian's life. Backed by McGillycuddy, Sword refused to pay

30. Endorsement on McGillycuddy to CIA, June 22, 1880 (OIALR, Roll 726).

the fine; at Pine Ridge, white concepts of justice were beginning to take precedence over native law-ways.[31]

The doctor and the captain of police had developed a fine working relationship, but before McGillycuddy could feel completely in control at Pine Ridge he had to depose Red Cloud. The chief supplied the pretext by writing a letter to President Arthur demanding the removal of the agent. McGillycuddy responded to the challenge by alerting his police, issuing carbines to an additional fifty friendly warriors, and ordering Red Cloud to appear before him. In a scene fraught with possibilities of violence, McGillycuddy lectured the old warrior and Captain Sword warned him against creating dissension.[32] The agent triumphed for the moment, but Red Cloud would be around for many more years to plague white administrators.

Although not sympathetic with tribal institutions of long standing, Dr. McGillycuddy appreciated their influence more than most Indian Service personnel, as is obvious in this perspicacious remark on the police:

> The Indians generally recognize the police authority, for from time immemorial there has existed among the Sioux and other tribes native soldier organizations, systematically governed by laws and regulations. Some of the strongest opposition encountered in endeavoring to organize the police force . . . was from these native organizations, for they at once recognized something in it strongly antagonistic to their ancient customs, namely, a force at the command of the white man opposed to their own.[33]

31. McGillycuddy to CIA, Oct. 7, 1879 (OIALR, Roll 131); *McGillycuddy: Agent*, pp. 123–26.
32. Doane Robinson, "The Education of Redcloud," *South Dakota Historical Collections, 12,* 176–78; McGillycuddy to CIA, Aug. 20, 1882 (OIALR, 15850, 1882).
33. AR of H. Price, 1881 (ser. 2018, p. 14).

At Standing Rock the agents faced problems even greater than McGillycuddy's. Orders to set up a police force were received there by Agent W. T. Hughes just before he resigned. After a brief interlude he was succeeded by J. A. Stephan who put fourteen policemen on the payroll in December 1878.[34] Arming and equipping the force was an immediate problem since the Indians at Standing Rock had been dismounted and disarmed during the campaign against the hostiles in 1876. Stephan finally was able to secure a few rifles in poor condition from the store of confiscated weapons at Fort Yates, the military post on the reservation.

The situation at Standing Rock was a classic example of friction between the military and civilian administrators of Indian affairs. Lieutenant Colonel W. P. Carlin, commanding Fort Yates, continued with Stephan a quarrel originating between Carlin and Agent Hughes. The civilians complained that the army officer interfered in Indian affairs by issuing hunting passes and weapons to Indians and by countenancing Sun Dances. The agents also accused the soldiers of debauching Indian women. Stephan charged that Colonel Carlin had his own representative among the Indians—Running Antelope—described by the agent as the "politician Indian of this Agency."[35] Stephan finally deposed Running Antelope as chief of a small band and placed his lodges under Thunder Hawk, a Progressive whom the agents trusted.

On several occasions Stephan requested the closing of Fort Yates, citing both the demoralization of the Indians by the garrison and the absence of any need for troops at Standing Rock. "I feel myself and the Government stores fully protected by my Indian police," Stephan told the Commissioner, "and therefore the presence of troops is not needed, but rather [is] a drawback to Indian civilization."[36] The re-

34. Police Pay Roll, Dec. 31, 1878 (OIALR, Roll 850).
35. Stephan to CIA, Feb. 21, 1880 (OIALR, Roll 851).
36. Stephan to CIA, June 12, 1880 (OIALR, Roll 852).

quest was forwarded through channels to General W. T. Sherman, who inspected Fort Yates in the summer of 1880. Before a meeting of settlers Sherman broached the subject of closing the military installation. When the settlers protested and expressed fear of the Indians if the troops were withdrawn, Agent Stephan rose to point out that nearly all the speakers who had expressed fear of the redskins were living with Indian women, legally or otherwise. Sherman, never a diplomatic individual, threatened to employ his scorched-earth tactics of Georgia fame and take away or burn every scrap of wood if Fort Yates were closed. He added insult to injury by interjecting that the Commissioner of Indian Affairs knew nothing of Indians, having seen only three or four, and those in a show.[37]

In this situation Stephan, like other agents, easily saw the merits of a force at his command that might free him from complete dependence on the military. In a dig at the latter, Stephan praised the Indian police for protecting their camps "from the nocturnal visits of drunken and lecherous soldiers."[38] His repeated complaints did achieve an expansion of his force to a total of thirty and their equipment with weapons supplied by the Indian Office. Apparently the agent did have sympathetic auditors in Washington, despite the obvious desire of Interior Department personnel to mute their disagreements with the War Department. Meanwhile, conditions at Standing Rock worsened.

Although the Standing Rock population was only about half that at Pine Ridge, it included Indians from four different Sioux tribes. In 1881 they were joined by nearly 3,000 recent hostiles and in May 1883 Sitting Bull himself was moved to Standing Rock where he immediately clashed with Agent James McLaughlin, Stephan's successor. Like Mc-

37. Stephan to CIA, Aug. 13, 1880, ibid.
38. AR of Stephan, 1880 (ser. 1959, p. 179).

Gillycuddy, McLaughlin was determined to rule his reservation but, unlike McGillycuddy and almost all other agents,
he was a veteran of the Indian Service and had come to
Standing Rock after ten years' experience in reservation administration. Appreciating the value of a police force, he
requested unsuccessfully that his be more than doubled to
cope with the influx of recent hostiles. McLaughlin had no
intention of permitting Sitting Bull and his allies to dominate
Standing Rock. The agent reported to Washington that the
Hunkpapa chief and medicine man wanted to be "big
chief."[39] When Sitting Bull refused to adopt the Progressive
posture, the agent turned to Gall, who with Crazy Horse had
led the final assault on Custer. Like Spotted Tail, Gall had
recognized the inevitable and had settled into the role of a
Progressive. In time he was to serve as a judge on the agency's
Court of Indian Offenses, and when the Ghost Dance gripped
the Sioux agencies in 1890 Gall remained aloof from the
tragedy enacted there.

The story of the Ghost Dance has been told often, and
the details are generally agreed upon.[40] The movement originated with Wovoka, a Paiute, who reported that he had been
taken to the spirit world where he had been given a message
for his Indian brethren. If the Indians would practice the
ceremonies known to the whites as the Ghost Dance, they
would prepare the way for the disappearance of the whites
and the return of the buffalo and other game. Comparable
to other messianic movements which had raised the hopes
of Indians being crushed by the white steamroller, the Ghost
Dance won converts from Oklahoma north to Canada. The

39. AR of McLaughlin, 1883 (ser. 2191, p. 106).
40. The standard account of the movement is James Mooney, *The
Ghost-Dance Religion and the Sioux Outbreak of 1890* (Washington,
1896). An excellent recent account is in Robert M. Utley, *The Last Days
of the Sioux Nation* (New Haven, 1963).

Southern Plains Indians got through the crisis without bloodshed, but at the Teton Sioux agencies it took Hotchkiss guns spewing fifty explosive shells a minute to convince the tribesmen that their specially blessed dance shirts were not proof against the white man's armament.

As usual, the police performance was of mixed quality. Those well trained, disciplined, and impervious to the influence of the Conservatives did well; others performed miserably. At Lower Brulé the agent anticipated trouble, and his police arrested and imprisoned seventeen of the ghost dancers. No troops were needed at this agency.[41]

At Cheyenne River only Big Foot's band defied the police, and they fled the reservation for a deadly rendezvous with the troops at Wounded Knee. Their agent credited the "faithful and excellent service of the police" as a factor in keeping his troubles to a minimum.[42]

The situation at Pine Ridge was complicated by the presence of an incompetent agent. D. F. Royer, assigned to this post in the middle of the Ghost Dance trouble, and the third man appointed to the reservation since McGillycuddy left in 1886, was inexperienced and easily intimidated. The alliances McGillycuddy had cultivated to contain Red Cloud had dissolved, and with them the quality of the Pine Ridge police force. Royer's successor called it "an utter and complete failure in case of an emergency."[43] Panicked by the possibilities of the Ghost Dance movement, Royer kept the telegraph wires to Washington hot with demands for troops.

His pleas were echoed, in calmer tones, by the agent at Rosebud. The police there had never been very efficient and Crow Dog, the former captain of police, was now a principal malcontent. Convinced he could not rely on the Indian force,

41. AR of A. P. Dixon, 1891 (ser. 2934, p. 403).
42. AR of Perain P. Palmer, 1891 (ser. 2934, p. 390).
43. AR of Chas. G. Penney, 1891 (ser. 2934, p. 409).

this agent also requested troops, and they were sent in to occupy Rosebud and adjoining Pine Ridge.

Meanwhile Agent McLaughlin was insisting his police could handle the situation at Standing Rock. Unlike Royer, McLaughlin wanted desperately to avoid the introduction of troops which he feared would cause a stampede of Indians from the reservation.

The agent's confidence in his police was not misplaced. On only one occasion did they fail to carry out their assignments. McLaughlin had learned of the arrival at Sitting Bull's camp of Kicking Bear, a Miniconjou from Cheyenne River and the principal medicine man of the Sioux Ghost Dance. Fearful of Kicking Bear's impact on the waverers, the agent ordered thirteen policemen to arrest the medicine man and expel him from the reservation. In the presence of the Ghost Dance rituals the resolution of the "metal breasts," as the Conservatives called them, faltered, and they contented themselves with asking Kicking Bear and other visitors to return to Cheyenne River. McLaughlin stated that Captain Crazy Walking and Lieutenant Chatka reported back in a "dazed condition."[44] But McLaughlin's medicine proved more powerful than Kicking Bear's, and Chatka volunteered to ensure that Kicking Bear did leave Standing Rock. With only two police to back him up, Chatka took the visiting ghost dancers into custody and delivered them to the boundary of the reservation. Years later McLaughlin recalled: "I cannot imagine a performance requiring more courage, from an Indian viewpoint, than that accomplished by Lieutenant Chatka that day."[45]

The success strengthened the agent's conviction he could handle the situation without troops. Nor did he welcome the

44. McLaughlin to CIA, Oct. 17, 1890 (ser. 2934, p. 329).
45. James McLaughlin, *My Friend the Indian* (Boston, 1910), p. 191.

aid of glamorous amateurs like Buffalo Bill Cody. Sitting Bull had starred in Cody's Wild West show, and Nelson Miles, commander of the Department of the Missouri, favored permitting Buffalo Bill an opportunity to persuade the Indian to leave the troubled area. McLaughlin managed to block that and insisted when the time was ripe his police could arrest the "polygamist, libertine, habitual liar, [and] active obstructionist," to use only some of the terms the agent applied to his principal problem.[46]

McLaughlin's plan called for delay until "cold weather cools the ardor of the dancers."[47] It also required that the arrest be made on a ration day, as Sitting Bull had been refusing to come to the agency for that function. If this scheme were employed, most of his band would be drawing rations forty miles from their hero when the police closed in on him. Also, the agent had been unobtrusively reinforcing the police camp nearest Sitting Bull's cabin and had almost doubled the size of his regular force.

The timing of the arrest was determined by the army and the old medicine man himself. The order to Lieutenant Colonel William F. Drum, commanding Fort Yates, the nearest military installation, was dated December 12. Drum was prepared to let the Indian police do the actual arresting but would provide two troops of cavalry to be in the vicinity if required. The colonel also agreed the attempt should be made on the next ration day, December 20. But Sitting Bull spoiled that timetable by making preparations to join over 2,000 Indians who had fled Pine Ridge, and Drum and McLaughlin feared the consequences if the inchoate mass of frightened but exalted Sioux rallied behind Sitting Bull. Orders to seize the old firebrand, therefore, were issued December 14.

46. McLaughlin to CIA (n. 44 above).
47. McLaughlin to Gen. Ruger, Dec. 6, 1890 (ser. 2934, p. 333).

They were received by Lieutenant Bull Head who, with Sergeants Shave Head, Little Eagle, Red Tomahawk, and Eagle Man led the thirty-nine policemen and four volunteers who joined them for the mission. At dawn the next morning they surrounded Sitting Bull's quarters, while a hundred troopers with Hotchkiss and Gatling guns took up positions a few miles away. Despite the camp's dogs, the police were inside Sitting Bull's cabin before he awakened. Told he was under arrest and ordered to prepare himself for the forty-mile ride to the agency, he began to dress. By the time the party was ready to leave the cabin, a crowd of over a hundred ghost dancers had gathered to see what was happening to their chief. In the half-light the Indians milled around, the women wailing, and agitators like Catch-the-Bear and Strikes-the-Kettle challenged the warriors to save their leader. Sitting Bull supplied the spark that ignited the explosion. Suddenly refusing to go any farther, he called out for help. Catch-the-Bear and Strikes-the-Kettle immediately opened fire, and in seconds there was general shooting. Lieutenant Bull Head and Sergeant Shave Head went down in the first exchange, but the lieutenant had fired a shot into Sitting Bull's body and Sergeant Red Tomahawk, behind the prisoner, shot him in the head. Sitting Bull died instantly. For a few desperate moments the police were almost overwhelmed as women joined their men and struck at the uniformed Indians with knives and clubs.

In the first burst of violence six policemen were killed and three wounded, two of them mortally. Eight of Sitting Bull's party died and several suffered wounds. The policemen first drove their attackers away and then took refuge in cabins where they were under long-range fire. Hawk Man No. 1, a policeman, had slipped away during the wild melee. He returned with the cavalry, and the combined fire of police and troops finally dispersed the ghost dancers.

The operation had not gone as McLaughlin had hoped, but the conduct of the police had been exemplary. One participant said the battle should be remembered in history "as showing the fidelity and loyalty of the Indian police in obeying orders and maintaining the integrity of the Government against their own people."[48] The cavalry commander was equally generous in his praise: "I can not too strongly commend the splendid courage and ability which characterized the conduct of the Indian police."[49] Herbert Welsh, president of the Indian Rights Association, spoke highly of the "moderation of the Indian police at the Sitting Bull fight" as contrasted with the "blind rage" he attributed to the troops participating in the Wounded Knee Massacre. Waxing lyric, Welsh suggested:

> It were well if the same chisel which recorded in "eternal bronze" the sad and patient nobility of Lincoln might also fashion some memorial to the humble heroes of Standing Rock! The genius of Thorwaldsen and the fidelity of the Swiss Guard breathe forever in the dying Lion of Lucerne. May not the genius of some American sculptor and the fidelity of the Indian police find similar expression?[50]

But not everyone was so ecstatic over the police performance. Secretary of the Interior John W. Noble feared adverse publicity for the Indian Service, and he tried to attribute the death of Sitting Bull solely to the War Department operation.[51] Noble did the police and their backers an injustice. McLaughlin's and Colonel Drum's premise that Sitting Bull

---

48. Extract of McLaughlin to CIA, Dec. 16, 1890 (ser. 2934, p. 337).
49. Ibid.
50. Herbert Welsh, "The Meaning of the Dakota Outbreak," *Scribner's* (April 1891), p. 451.
51. Utley, *Last Days of the Sioux Nation*, p. 168.

had to be prevented from joining the Sioux in the Bad Lands could not be gainsaid, and it was fortunate that the army did not have to perform the unpleasant chore. Sitting Bull's band would have scattered at the first rumor of troops, and more than one Wounded Knee Massacre would have resulted. The entire Ghost Dance episode demonstrated that a disciplined and trained police force could reduce an agent's dependence on the army and minimize the crises that arose. Indeed, the whole Sioux experiment with police generally justified the policy.

6. Courts of Indian Offenses

THE INSTRUCTIONS to the agents to organize police forces, sent from Washington by the Commissioner in 1878, did not make specific provision for the trial and punishment of offenders. Not until 1883 did the Secretary of the Interior authorize Courts of Indian Offenses, and in the interim, left to their own ingenuity, the agents resorted to a variety of expedients. The most common solution was for the agent himself to act as judge, or he might delegate the duty to one of his white subordinates or to a trusted Indian. This was in line with a course of action suggested several times by Commissioners of Indian Affairs and Secretaries of the Interior,[1] who envisioned the agents as justices of the peace or the tribes administering law through elected governments. If neither of these courses was practicable, there remained the possibility of using the nearest federal courts. The extra burden for the federal judiciary might require that additional courts be created in Indian Territory. The Senate was considering in 1882 one such bill that would have provided an all-Indian jury for full-bloods on trial, and "a jury composed of one-half of persons of mixed Indian and other blood where one of the litigants belongs to that other blood, or of one-half negro or mulattoes where a negro or mulatto

1. For example, see AR of Jas. Harlan, 1865 (ser. 1248, p. ix); Henry E. Fritz, *The Movement for Indian Assimilation, 1860–1890* (Philadelphia, 1963), pp. 216–17.

is a litigant."[2] Behind this unique proposal, and others more practical, was the conviction that additional courts must be made available to inhabitants of Indian Territory if they were to progress in civilization. Members of Congress were strangely unmoved by this logic. Observed one member of the Indian Service: "Our legislators here have much faith in law for white men; I wish it were possible to persuade them that it is equally beneficial to Indians."[3]

On a few reservations the agents experimented with permitting the tribesmen to elect their own justices. One of the more ambitious of these efforts occurred at the Yakima Agency where R. H. Milroy presided. A veteran of the Civil War, he was commonly referred to as General Milroy, which gave him rank of a sort over the numerous "Majors" managing reservations in the post-Civil War era.

Before coming to Yakima the general had served for ten years at another reservation and there had delegated the judicial function in criminal cases to his chief of police, and in civil cases to a tribal council. Moving to his new post he found himself devoting too much time to adjudicating minor disputes. Milroy's response was to divide the reservation into five judicial districts and provide for the election of judges. The problem of the illiteracy of the electorate was overcome by assigning colors to the candidates. Instead of marking his ballot the voter simply chose the one of the proper hue and deposited it in the ballot box. The judge so elected handled the cases for his district. Appeals from his decision could be carried to a court of three justices, and beyond that to Milroy

2. *Congressional Record,* 13 (5) (1882), 4511 CIA H. Price suggested that when Dakota and New Mexico became states their courts should be given jurisdiction over the Indian populations of those states. AR of Price, 1883 (ser. 2191, p. 8).

3. AR of Wm. Nicholson, 1876 (ser. 1749, p. 477).

himself: "I am the supreme court."[4] Obviously proud of his accomplishments, he related them, in those rather patronizing tones reformers reserved for Indians, Negroes, and half-witted children, to friends of the Indian at a Lake Mohonk conference. Milroy also assured the Commissioner of Indian Affairs that "justice is now about as speedily and as rightly administered on this reservation as among the whites outside."[5]

Agent initiative partially accounted for the creation of a court among the Osages, who had expressed an interest in emulating their neighbors, the Five Civilized Tribes. In 1881 the Osages drafted a constitution based on that of the Cherokees, providing for supreme, circuit, and lower courts. The judges were nominated by the Osage Governor, confirmed by the Council, and served two-year terms at annual salaries of $200 drawn from poll-tax receipts.[6] An accused person did not have the privilege of facing a jury of his peers and, if found guilty, he might be publicly whipped. Despite these shortcomings, the Osage court system performed well for many years.

Where geography made it practical, reservation suspects were tried in federal courts. But this occurred seldom, as the nearest federal court was usually many miles distant. Witnesses to crimes were hard to locate when testifying was such an expensive and time-consuming business. At Pine Ridge in 1880 Agent McGillycuddy had a convenient arrangement for his white suspects. His chief clerk was also a United States Commissioner before whom the suspect was

4. Report of the Board of Indian Commissioners, 1884 (ser. 2287, p. 725).
5. AR of Milroy, 1885 (ser. 2379, p. 430).
6. Frank F. Finney, Sr., "Progress in the Civilization of the Osage, and Their Government," *Chronicles of Oklahoma* (Spring 1962), pp. 9–11.

arraigned. The Commissioner would then decide, without their having to leave the reservation, whether the prisoner should be tried by the federal court at Deadwood—"going over the road to Deadwood," in reservation parlance.[7]

Despite the need for courts, as seen in these makeshift judicial arrangements, the Courts of Indian Offenses appear to have originated in a random reform impulse of Secretary of the Interior H. M. Teller. Elected to the Senate from Colorado in 1876, Teller, as a spokesman of a frontier state, took an active interest in Indian affairs. His bias was reflected in his defense of the butchering of Cheyenne women and children by the Colorado militia in the infamous Sand Creek Massacre. On other issues his position was rather surprising. Western politicians usually found it easy to support allotment proposals, since this would break up the reservations and facilitate their constituents' acquisition of land. Senator Teller, perhaps because his constituents included many ranchers who preferred to lease from venal reservation officials and tribal leaders, consistently opposed the principle of allotment. He forecast with considerable accuracy the dire results of such legislation on Indian landholdings. Furthermore, in Senate debate he inveighed against off-reservation boarding schools, another popular policy, and emphasized the necessity of measures calculated to speed acculturation of Indians on their own reservations.

Appointed Secretary of the Interior in 1882, Teller had been in office only a few months when he reminded the Commissioner of Indian Affairs of the persistence on some reservations of "certain of the old heathenish dances; such as the sun-dance, scalp-dance, &c." The Secretary held they were not mere social functions but "are intended and calculate to stimulate the warlike passions." The veteran of

7. AR of Geo. LeRoy Brown, 1892 (ser. 3088, p. 456).

the Plains troubles of the Sixties and Seventies described
this scene:

> The warrior recounts his deeds of daring, boasts of his
> inhumanity in the destruction of his enemies, and his
> treatment of the female captives, in language that
> ought to shock even a savage ear. The audience assents
> approvingly to his boasts of falsehood, deceit, theft,
> murder, and rape, and the young listener is informed
> that this and this only is the road to fame and renown.
> the result is the demoralization of the young.[8]

Secretary Teller likewise thought something should be done
about plural marriages, the influence of medicine men, and
the destruction of the property of deceased persons. He did
not suggest punishing Indians for polygamous arrangements
already made. Teller in previous debate in the Senate on
this subject had said that he would settle for "what the early
Christian Church allowed to its converts. . . . I do not think
these Indians ought to be required to put away their wives.
They ought to be prohibited from marrying any more." Like
some modern Treasury watchdogs, he purported to see in
the government-aid programs an explanation for the increase in polygamous households: "the more numerous the
family the greater the number of the rations allowed."[9]

Teller concluded his letter with a request that Commissioner Hiram Price formulate a set of rules to end the
objectionable practices. Three weeks later Price, an Iowan
and active Methodist, was happy to comply. His first proposals were rejected as too expensive since they involved
hiring Indian judges. On March 30 the Commissioner forwarded a solution—assign to the top three officers of each
police force the additional uncompensated duty of judge

8. AR of Teller, 1883 (ser. 2190, p. xi).
9. *Congressional Record, 11* (2) (1881), 1028.

of a Court of Indian Offenses. Price assured his superior that if his proposal were implemented rigorously it could "well accomplish the ultimate abolishment of the evil practices."[10]

Accordingly, Courts of Indian Offenses were established where the agent and the Commissioner of Indian Affairs concluded they were practical and desirable—that is, for all Indians but the Five Civilized Tribes, the Indians of New York, the Osage, the Pueblos, and the Eastern Cherokees, all of which had recognized tribal governments. The peak of their activity was reached around 1900 when about two thirds of the agencies had their own courts. Some agencies never established a court, others experimented with them only briefly. The niggardliness, of congressional appropriations for the support of courts limited the number that could function at any given time. The final decisions on where the courts were to be lay with the Commissioner of Indian Affairs who made the judgment, as an Acting Commissioner expressed it in 1891, "as it may appear the good of the Indian Service requires."[11]

Commissioner Price compiled a set of rules for Courts of Indian Offenses; these were approved on April 10, 1883, by Secretary Teller and circulated to the agents. They provided guidelines for court organization and procedure and an abbreviated criminal and civil code. In recruiting judges the agents were directed to seek out Indians "intelligent, honest, and upright, and of undoubted integrity." Aside from that the only qualification required was that the prospective jurist not be a polygamist.

The court was to meet at least twice a month. The grant of jurisdiction was sweeping; it could rule "upon all such questions as may be presented to it for consideration by the

10. Price to Teller, March 30, 1883 (OIALB, vol. 39).

11. R. V. Belt to Charles A. Bartholomew, March 16, 1891 (Southern Ute Agency Files).

agent." The rules specifically assigned to the courts such
offenses as the dances which had originally aroused Teller's
ire, plural marriage, and interference of medicine men with
the civilization program. Jurisdiction was also granted over
the theft or destruction of property, even if the "party
charged was at the time a 'mourner' and thereby justified in
taking or destroying the property in accordance with the
custom or rites of the tribe." Payment for the privilege of
cohabiting with a female was listed as an offense. Intoxication and the liquor traffic were specifically assigned to the
court's purview, as were misdemeanors and civil suits to
which Indians were party. In general, "The civil jurisdiction
of such court shall be the same as that of a Justice of
the Peace in the State or Territory where such a court is
located."[12]

It was recognized then and later that there was at best
a shaky legal foundation for these tribunals in the generally acknowledged authority of the Department of the
Interior to supervise Indian affairs. In 1886 Commissioner
J. D. C. Atkins referred to the necessity of putting them on a
"legal basis."[13] Four years later Commissioner T. J. Morgan
could allude to the now "quasi-legal basis" for the Courts
of Indian Offenses, which had been maintained for eight
years "without money, legislative authority, or precedent."[14]
The Board of Indian Commissioners in 1891 called them
"so-called courts of Indian Offenses" and indicated they were
"more in the nature of courts martial than civil courts, and
practically register the decrees of the Indian agent."[15] Al-

12. Rules for Courts of Indian Offenses, April 10, 1883 (OIALB,
vol. 39).
13. AR of Atkins, 1886 (ser. 2467, p. 103).
14. AR of Morgan, 1890 (ser. 2841, p. lxxxiii).
15. Report of the Board of Indian Commissioners, 1892 (ser. 2934,
p. 1102).

though payment of the judges was authorized in 1888, Congress was unable to free the courts from their reputation as tools of the Interior Department.

The failure to provide salaries for judges when the Indian courts were established had necessitated that the police double as judges. The disadvantages of this were obvious. The officer arrested a suspect and brought him to the agency office, changed hats, and passed judgment on him. Agents recognized the potential for injustice in this system, one reporting: "Our most active and vigilant police . . . make poor judges."[16] Securing responsible Indians to work without pay, however, was difficult. The experiences of the agents on the Great Sioux Reserve were typical. Only Standing Rock had a functioning court by 1886, and there two of the judges were police officers. Elsewhere they refused to sit without compensation, and at Pine Ridge Sergeant Standing Soldier spelled out his reasons to his agent:

> Father, we have served the Government and our own people faithfully for five years. In protecting life and property and adopting the white man's ways we have risked our lives and incurred the enmity of many of our people, and for that service we, as commissioned officers of the police receive but $8 per month and furnish our own horse. . . . Now, to act as judges over our own people and condemn them to punishment when necessary will still further endanger our lives and increase their enmity, and we will be paid nothing in addition therefor.[17]

Permitting the judges to draw salaries from funds fed by fines they had levied was tried at some reservations, for

16. AR of Joseph Emery, 1887 (ser. 2542, p. 269).
17. AR of McGillycuddy, 1884 (ser. 2287, p. 84).

example the Nez Percé and Yakima, but the danger of
degrading justice was patent.

As agent after agent reported his inability to recruit
judges willing to serve without pay, the Indian Office renewed its efforts to persuade Congress to underwrite the
policy. Only seven months after the courts were inaugurated,
the Commissioner in a burst of optimism requested an
appropriation of $50,000 to pay monthly salaries of $20.
The following year he again requested the sum, arguing that
good judges could not be recruited because the best qualified
"are unwilling to leave their farms and business occupations
when they know their only reward may be a loss of influence
and popularity among the tribe."[18]

Not until June 1888 did Congress see fit to appropriate
for judges' salaries, and then only one tenth of the sum
requested. Seeking advice on how to expend this $5,000 the
Commissioner circularized the agents for their opinions of
the courts and the compensation they would propose for
judges. The Commissioner concluded from his responses
that $10 to $12 per month would be adequate, but even this
pittance he could not provide. That year the judges received
salaries ranging from $3 to $8 per month, but for only
seven months of the year.[19] The next year the same general
situation prevailed, but in July 1890 Congress doubled the
appropriation. This was not done without a struggle. Senator
Francis M. Cockrell of Missouri tried to hold the sum to
$7,500. Contrary to all the evidence available, Cockrell
insisted the judges had performed faithfully without compensation, and the Senator feared the corrupting influence
of a salary. "It will degenerate into compensation alone,"
he warned, "detached from any honor or any respect, simply

18. AR of H. Price, 1884 (ser. 2287, p. 8).
19. AR of Morgan, 1890 (ser. 2841, p. lxxxiv).

for the compensation."[20] This possibility did not frighten Senator Orville H. Platt of Connecticut, who preferred enlarging the network of Indian courts to instituting a much more ambitious and expensive system preferred by the reformers and the Office of Indian Affairs. Platt's logic prevailed, and in the 1890s the Courts of Indian Offenses appeared on more reservations; the income of the judges rose, but never to the level the Commissioners would have liked. In 1891 most judges made $10 per month, but a few received only $3; as late as 1904 the average monthly salary was only $7.

Inadequate pay was only one problem. Like the police, judges had to be selected from the ranks of the Progressives, preferably full-bloods to command respect, and it helped if the various bands at an agency were represented. As a Ponca agent observed, "By distributing these offices more generally in the tribe [it] would render an adequate support and be more civilizing in character."[21]

Picking the best-qualified judges was as difficult a task as an agent had: he must understand the unofficial power structure existing on his reservation, be able to fathom personality traits of an alien culture, and be sure his candidates would meet with approval in Washington. The agent for the Sacs and Foxes of Iowa admitted his failure:

> This band of Indians is controlled by about 10 persons who have all the say and whose words are law, in a measure. To select judges from them would accomplish nothing, nor do I think they would understand the meaning or jurisdiction of the office. To select judges from outside the chieftainship would be an impossibility, because the Indians would be afraid to act.[22]

20. *Congressional Record,* 21 (8) (1890), 7605.
21. D. J. M. Wood to CIA, Oct. 3, 1889 (Ponca LB).
22. AR of W. R. Lesser, 1890 (ser. 2841, p. 105).

Nor was he alone; many other agents had similar problems. The Sioux at Rosebud in 1891 were divided into two factions, membership in which was determined by whether the Indian had been friendly or hostile during the Ghost Dance trouble. Still another cleavage, between the older and younger men, further confused and complicated the situation.[23]

Whistlepoosum, a judge of the Court of Indian Offenses of the Lower Spokanes in 1888, met and overcame one difficulty plaguing Indian justices—dealing without bias with one's relatives. Many judges were unable to achieve the Olympian detachment necessary. Family ties were very strong in Indian communities, and one was expected to support one's relatives. But Whistlepoosum had his own son arrested and tried on a charge of attempted murder. The accused was found innocent when only hearsay evidence was introduced against him. In his closing remarks, the father and judge declared that, had his son been guilty, sentence would have been carried out. That a son would even be tried in his father's court suggests something about the free and easy administration of justice by the Courts of Indian Offenses.[24]

Persistence of the "heathenish" practices which had so disturbed Secretary Teller hampered selection of judges at some reservations. A new agent for the Cheyennes and Arapahoes

23. J. George Wright to CIA, March 30, 1891 (OIALR, 12456, 1891).
24. AR of Richard D. Gwyder, 1888 (ser. 2637, p. 223). Francis E. Leupp tells the story of how the superintendent of a West Coast reservation coped with the problem of favoritism. He called in his judges and told them of Brutus, the Roman jurist who sentenced his own son to death, directing his remarks to one judge notorious for favoring his relatives. Several days later the superintendent was called to his door to receive a prisoner, bound hand and foot, and delivered up by the particular object of his lecture. The judge offered the superintendent his pistol, exclaiming, "Dis my nephew—me ketch 'm dlunk—you shoot 'm! Me Blutus!" Leupp, *The Indian and His Problem* (New York, 1910), pp. 243–44.

advocated allowing an established court to expire when a judge informed him that "polygamy, purchases of women, and taking property on the death of an Indian, or one of his family, was a custom of Indians and if I interfered I would get myself into trouble."[25] Judge Pawnee Man tried to explain to his agent that God had intended the Indians to enjoy as many wives as they wished.

At Quinault Agency in Washington Territory no judge would serve in a case involving medicine men, for fear of their lethal power.[26] Feather-in-the-Ear and other Sioux Conservatives at Yankton petitioned for the removal of their judges because the appointees were Christians and could not be controlled by the Conservatives.[27] Religious beliefs were also a factor at the Crow Creek, Standing Rock, Yankton, and Menomini agencies. The Crow Creek judges were chosen from various Christian denominations to try to satisfy all factions.[28] At Standing Rock, after the court had been functioning for several years, Protestant Indians complained that their Catholic brethren controlled it and were discriminating against them.[29] The Menomini judicial system was weakened by the membership of two of its judges in the Mitawin Lodge, one of the religious cults that emerged as the Indians struggled to maintain their identity.[30] Religion, which once had knit Indian societies more closely together, was now proving to be just another force hastening their dissolution.

As an alternative to the onerous task of weighing religious

25. Charles F. Ashley to CIA, March 19, 1891 (OIALR, 11021, 1891).

26. AR of Charles Willoughby, 1886 (ser. 2467, p. 459).

27. J. F. Kinney to CIA, Aug. 1, 1887 (OIALR, 20677, 1887).

28. AR of James H. Stephens, 1900 (ser. 4101, p. 374).

29. James Garvie to CIA, March 11, 1901 (OIALR, 15840, 1901).

30. Felix M. Keesing, *The Menomini Indians of Wisconsin* (Philadelphia, 1939), p. 191.

and other factors in selecting judges, an occasional agent would leave it to the Indians. Divided into three voting districts, the Fort Peck Agency was the scene of "electioneering, log-rolling, wire-pulling, and all the etcetera of an election in civilized life."[31] The Siletz Reservation, in the midst of a campaign to elect judges, even produced charges of vote buying.[32] When the Sioux at Crow Creek indicated a desire to elect their judges, the agent endorsed it as a way of getting rid of the hereditary chiefs. The Commissioner approved and indicated a procedure to be followed: only adult males could vote, judges and clerks to conduct the election were to be appointed by the agent, and the final result should be subject to the approval of the Commissioner.[33] The Indian Office was not prepared yet to entrust tribesmen with a completely democratic process.

All things considered, the rather haphazard selection system worked well. Unfortunately, one of the judges most frequently mentioned did not reflect credit on the system. History is indebted for his story to Fletcher Cowart, Agent of the Mescalero Apaches. As Cowart related it the Mescalero judge was diverted from the path of duty by the sight of a full bottle of liquor introduced in evidence in the trial of a drunk. After imposing sentence the judge adjourned the court and asked the chief of police for the liquid evidence. He was refused, and he humbled himself to offer to share the prisoner's jail sentence of a week if he could satisfy his desperate thirst. "This affords a fair idea of the importance, impartiality, and dignity of a court of Indian offenses," concluded Cowart sourly.[34]

31. AR of C. R. A. Scobey, 1892 (ser. 3088, p. 299).
32. AR of T. J. Buford, 1893 (ser. 3210, p. 271).
33. W. W. Anderson to CIA, June 23, 1890 (OIALR, 19516, 1890); CIA to Anderson, July 2, 1890 (OIALB, vol. 201).
34. AR of Fletcher J. Cowart, 1886 (ser. 2467, p. 419).

This was a patently unfair condemnation of the system, but the almost equally well-known portrait of a Blackfeet Judge, Shorty White-Grass, is probably too flattering. It originated with a report of Dr. Merrill E. Gates, a prominent defender of Indian rights and a member of the Board of Indian Commissioners, who made a tour of reservations in 1899. At the Blackfeet Agency he observed the Indian court trying the case of *Cowbedding* v. *Cowbedding.* The presiding judge was Shorty White-Grass, who shared the bench with Little Plume and Wolf Tail. The parties to the case, man and wife, had quarreled, the man had struck the woman with a porcelain dipper, and the police were called in. No formal charges had been filed, and the court was not being asked to pass upon points of law but to hear both sides and assign blame.

In their native tongue the couple related their individual versions of the domestic dispute. The woman, who Gates obviously found attractive, was colorfully attired in a white dress with red trim, a yellow-striped red handkerchief over her head, a scarf of red, yellow, and blue around her neck, and over all a blue and white blanket. Several brass bracelets and rings weighted her slender hands and fingers and testified to her worth to her husband. She told of having "jossed" him in front of some of his male friends, exposing him to embarrassment and ridicule. She further related that on his return home he had refused to eat the supper she had prepared and, after an exchange of unpleasantries and the blow with the dipper, he had threatened to divorce her by the tribal custom of driving her from the cabin. His mother intervened at this point and the following morning the couple separately called in the police.

Cowbedding, a handsome Indian with long black hair, wore a blue suit and moccasins. He told essentially the same tale and with the same quiet dignity and lack of emotion as his wife. He explained his blow as his reaction to her striking their small child and expressed regret for the whole incident.

After the judges had deliberated, White-Grass handed down the court's opinion. It denounced the domestic squabble but took into consideration the absence of any serious cuts and bruises and advised reconciliation in lieu of punishment of the parties. Gates was much impressed by White-Grass's dignity, eloquence, and logic. The judge was a striking figure: only four feet, eight inches tall, he had a huge head atop a powerful torso and enunciated in tones "which would fill easily and well the chamber of our House of Representatives at its noisiest." A green parrot frequently rested on the judge's left arm, and some suspected it of whispering words of wisdom to him. Presumably the parrot did not aid in rendering judgment in *Cowbedding* v. *Cowbedding,* but Gates termed the judge's performance "as kindly a mingling of paternal and neighborly advice with the administration of rudimentary justice as one could ever hope to hear."[35] Like the colonial judge who disregarded precedents with a blithe, "Every tub must stand on its own bottom,"[36] White-Grass and his fellow justices were not addicted to historical jurisprudence. They settled each case on its own merits.

The relaxed informality Merrill Gates observed in the Blackfeet court was typical. The original instructions of the Commissioner had merely said that "the practice in such civil cases shall conform as nearly as practicable to the rules governing the practice of Justices of the Peace."[37] In 1892 new instructions to the agents were more specific. They directed the judges to recruit from among the Indians a clerk

35. Report of the Board of Indian Commissioners, 1899 (ser. 3916, pp. 326–27).

36. Quoted in Daniel J. Boorstin, *The Americans* (New York, 1964), p. 201.

37. Rules for Courts of Indian Offenses (n. 12 above).

who would "maintain a docket" and preserve a "proper record" of each case and discharge other duties normally performed by court clerks. The new instructions also provided that procedures should conform generally to accepted practices in state and territorial courts.[38]

Despite these instructions, the operations of the Court of Indian Offenses continued to resemble only in broad outline court procedures of white communities. Agents were not appointed for their legal training, and they found it impossible to locate judges and clerks with the desired background. Indian graduates of Carlisle and Hampton frequently served as clerks, or even as attorneys where the agent permitted them to practice in court. This was one of the very few opportunities afforded returned students to put to use on the reservation any of their language skills or knowledge of the white man's way, and they eagerly seized it. Although a brief record might be kept in English, proceedings normally were conducted in the native tongues, since it was a rare occasion when the officials and all parties spoke English well.[39]

At an Oregon agency there was a curious digression from the usual procedures. There the court consisted of three judges, only one of whom was permanent. For each new case before the court the other two judges were selected from among the police, the plaintiff and the defendant each choosing one.[40]

It was this relaxed approach to judicial procedure which led to some of the more perceptive comments on the Courts of Indian Offenses. Clark Wissler witnessed the workings of

38. AR of T. J. Morgan, 1892 (ser. 3088, pp. 27–31).

39. At the Cheyenne River Agency in 1891, the court record was kept in the Dakota language. AR of Perain P. Palmer, 1891 (ser. 2934, p. 390).

40. AR of T. Jay Buford, 1892 (ser. 3088, p. 416).

a court around 1900 and commented on the dignity of the judges, yet the absence of protocol: "Common sense rather than hoary ritualism was the order of the day."[41] The agent at the Fort Hall Reservation in 1890 pointed out, with unconscious irony, a concomitant of this unconcern with form: "No guilty party ever escapes punishment on account of a technicality of the law."[42] A similar virtue was detected by another member of the Indian Service in absence of attorneys: "No lawyers perplex the judges."[43]

Greater use of attorneys for the defense perhaps would have helped systematize court judgments. The original instructions in 1883 and the version in 1892 specified a range of penalties for infractions of the various rules administered by the Courts of Indian Offenses. Withholding rations, fining, and imprisonment were the standard punishments. In the 1892 rules they ranged from up to five days' imprisonment for failure to do road work and up to six months for medicine men convicted a second time of interfering with the civilization programs. The principal innovation of the 1892 revision smacked of the provisions of the Black Codes designed to force ex-slaves into employment in the immediate post-Civil War years. It provided: "That if an Indian refuses or neglects to adopt habits of industry, or to engage in civilized pursuits or employments, but habitually spends his time in idleness and loafing, he shall be deemed a vagrant," and punished accordingly.[44] This is an excellent illustration of how the government hoped to use the power inherent in the Indian police and Courts of Indian Offenses to coerce acculturation.

Imprisonment and withholding rations were sentences

41. Wissler, *Indian Cavalcade*, p. 160.
42. AR of S. G. Fisher, 1890 (ser. 2841, p. 77).
43. AR of John H. Waugh, 1890 (ser. 2934, p. 317).
44. AR of T. J. Morgan, 1892 (ser. 3088, p. 30).

handed down less often than fines and hard labor. Families deprived of rations simply looked to their relatives and neighbors; in an Indian camp no one went hungry if there was food in other households. Although Indian societies were long on sharing, they were short on penal facilities. In the absence of a jail for the Paiutes in 1888, culprits were chained to a tree;[45] but the usual solution was to convert an extra room at agency headquarters into a cell or to use the guardhouse if an army post were handy and the commanding officer cooperative.

Whether to an army guardhouse or to a reservation lockup, it was seldom that a court sentenced an Indian to an extended confinement. Sixty- and ninety-day sentences were reported, but closer examination reveals that the prisoner probably passed his days working around the agency and spent the nights with his family. If he were locked up, jail breaking was not much of a risk. Except for those corrupted by contact with whites, Indian prisoners were usually remarkably amenable and cooperative. There was not even a lock on the jail that housed the Sioux malefactors at Devils Lake in North Dakota in 1898.[46]

The courts considerably swelled the labor force available to agents. The predominantly Snohomish prisoners at Tulalip Agency were sentenced to do about 600 days of road work one year, 815 the next, and 1,366 the third. The steady rise in the sentences reflects a growing appreciation by the agent of the virtue of hard labor over fines, rather than a spectacular increase in drunkenness, which did bring most of the Snohomish before the court. Nor was it a chain-gang type of

45. AR of W. D. C. Gibson, 1888 (ser. 2637, p. 183).
46. AR of F. O. Getchell, 1898 (ser. 3757, p. 222). A Yankton agent reported that defendants in trials of the local Court of Indian Offenses did not contest the charges if they were guilty. "It would be considered cowardly to deny them," he said of the Indian reaction. AR of J. F. Kinney, 1886 (ser. 2467, p. 317).

operation. A schedule of different varieties of road work had been drawn up (ditching, grading, crowning), and how much of each constituted a reasonable eight hours' work. The prisoner was assigned a particular task and it was up to him to get it done before the next session of court. A supervisor would inspect it when the prisoner indicated it was ready and, if it passed muster, the Indian's debt to society had been paid.[47]

Drunkenness probably brought more Indians before the courts than any other offense. Killing a pig or cow which had invaded his vegetable garden occasionally got an Indian into trouble, ironically, since having a vegetable patch to be invaded was evidence of progress in civilization. Of the particular practices Secretary Teller sought to banish, extra-marital relations were most often before the court, and actions involving medicine men and dances the least. Many agents probably found themselves in the situation of an official administering the Otoes. His charges refused to abandon their medicine men, saying that it would simply mean more of them would die, because the agency physician refused to make calls. The agent agreed and did not press the matter.[48]

Tribal dancing was a sensitive topic, and in response to an inquiry a Commissioner ruled that "modest" dances performed by the Pueblos did not come under the ban.[49] How thoroughly the interdict could be applied can be seen on the Great Sioux Reserve. The last Sun Dance, a vital ceremony in the life of the Plains Indians, was held at Pine Ridge in 1883.[50]

47. AR of Charles M. Buchanan, 1902 (ser. 4458, p. 361); 1903 (ser. 4645, p. 338); 1904 (ser. 4798, p. 363).
48. J. P. Woolsey to CIA, May 8, 1894 (Ponca LB).
49. CIA to Pedro Sanchez, June 27, 1883 (Pueblo File).
50. Utley, *Last Days of the Sioux Nation*, p. 32.

A wise agent obviously would use a little common sense in determining which dances were harmful. It was more difficult to dodge the problem of sex relations outside the limits approved by white society, and court records abound with cases of that nature. Adultery, rape, polygamy, cohabitation, licentiousness, bastardy, and fornication are some of the case labels appearing most frequently in court records. The persistence of native mores seemed particularly pronounced in this area. A Sioux agent complained of an Indian who dressed like a white man, mingled freely with whites, and otherwise had made considerable progress in civilization, and yet was willing to accept a horse in satisfaction for the rape of his wife.[51] That an Indian society might have evolved this type of settlement as meeting its needs presumably did not occur to the agent. Some judges took a more pragmatic view of such matters; for example, a Chippewa convicted of attempted rape was fined heavily and the money turned over to the object of his attentions.[52] This was substantially in line with Chippewa practice, but Blackstone could not have provided a precedent for it.

On the Sioux reservations the courts were employed to help disarm those Indians who still caused nightmares in lonely farmhouses. Judge Abraham No Heart and his colleagues at Cheyenne River in 1891 were no longer levying cash fines—all fines were payable in guns. The Standing Rock court collected fines of seventy-four rifles and five revolvers in one year. Agent McLaughlin was particularly pleased with the treatment accorded the "conceited and obstinate Sitting Bull," who had attacked Shell King with a tomahawk. The weapon was confiscated, as was the knife with which Shell King defended himself.[53]

51. AR of J. F. Kinney, 1887 (ser. 2542, p. 136).
52. AR of E. W. Brenner, 1903 (ser. 4645, p. 233).
53. AR of James McLaughlin, 1887 (ser. 2542, pp. 134–35).

The court before which Sitting Bull and Shell King were haled in 1887 was presided over by John Grass, chief of the Blackfeet Sioux, and two police officers. Grass remained on the court for several years, serving, after the officers gave way to regular judges, with Gall of the Hunkpapa and Standing Soldier of the Lower Yanktonais. Grass was a Progressive and a full-blood, known among the Indians as Charging Bear. The chairman of a commission to the Sioux in 1889 described him as "an intellectual giant in comparison with other Indians."[54] His willingness to use his influence to push a treaty to open a large section of the Sioux reserve to settlement contributed to his stature in the eyes of the whites and won him the enmity of Sitting Bull.

John Grass had clearly been typed a white man's Indian. The Comanche mixed-blood, Quanah Parker, was a tribesman and judge who more successfully essayed the role of mediator between the races without becoming a pawn in the hands of the agent. But both he and John Grass represented a solution to a problem in reservation administration. Like the police, the Indian judges were not exactly what any particular faction concerned with Indian policy would have preferred. Certainly Secretary Teller hoped his Courts of Indian Offenses would be more energetic in rooting out remnants of tribal culture than was to be the case. Agents, meanwhile, were happy to have a court with some legal standing to which they could refer their quota of petty thieves, quarreling neighbors, and bickering married couples. When, after several years' delay, Congress finally appropriated funds to pay the judges' salaries, a major step had been taken in making the courts effective. The necessary division between police and judicial functions could now be maintained. The very small salaries alone, however, do

54. AR of James McLaughlin, 1889 (ser. 2725, p. 169).

not explain why tribesmen of the stature of Quanah Parker sought seats on the courts. Where agents chose to share their power and authority, they could make such positions attractive to any politically minded Indian.

7. Judge Quanah Parker

THE FIRST COURT OF INDIAN OFFENSES for the Kiowas and Comanches opened in 1886.[1] A decade had passed since the last of these famed Plains warriors had come to terms at Fort Sill. In the intervening years Kiowa chiefs Kicking Bird, Lone Wolf, and Satanta had died—Satanta by leaping from the window of a Texas prison and Kicking Bird possibly from poisoning by tribal enemies. Death had not taken a comparable toll among the Comanche leadership, but in both tribes the old Conservatives were being shunted aside in favor of Indians more amenable to the agents.

The deterioration of these once proud nomads was a pitiful thing. In the late 1870s they still sought permission to leave the reservation to hunt buffalo, but by 1886 the mighty herds were things of the past. Kiowa and Comanche warriors now subsisted on rations provided under the 1867 Treaty of Medicine Lodge. Efforts to civilize them availed little. As late as 1890 the average tribesman lived in a tipi, of canvas now rather than buffalo hide, spoke little or no English, wore his hair long, and clung to the warrior tradition that regarded agriculture as woman's work.

What was referred to frequently as the Kiowa Agency at Anadarko actually comprised nine tribes. The Comanches in 1886 were the most numerous—about 1,600; the Kiowas

1. Much of this material has appeared as "Quanah Parker, Indian Judge," in K. Ross Toole, et al., eds., *Probing the American West,* and *El Palacio* (Spring 1962).

accounted for over 1,100; the remaining seven tribes totaled about 1,300.[2] They occupied nearly four million acres in the southwestern corner of what is now Oklahoma, bounded on the north by the Canadian River, on the south and west by Texas, and on the east by the Chickasaw Nation. While not so harassed by white intruders as the Indians to their east, the reservation had its quota of squaw men, fugitives, and rustlers. It had more than its quota of Texas cowboys and longhorns. The vacant pastures of the Indians proved more of a temptation than Texans could resist, and their herds waded Red River to be "lost" on tribal land for weeks at a time.

Keeping the reservation clear of Texas longhorns had been a principal assignment of the police force established at the agency in 1878. Conservative opposition and lack of weapons militated against the effectiveness of the force in its early years, but by 1886 the agent could describe the police as "gradually becoming more efficient."[3]

What was lacking now was a court before which those accused of minor crimes might appear. Until one was created, those suspected of certain crimes were arraigned before a United States commissioner in Wichita Falls and could ultimately be tried at Fort Smith. If held for trial by the commissioner, the Indian went to jail, since he could never furnish bail. In 1878 several Comanche chiefs, including Quanah Parker, protested the inconvenience of having to travel to Fort Smith,[4] but nothing was done until eight years later. In 1886 Captain J. Lee Hall established the first Court of Indian Offenses with Quanah as one of the judges. Under Hall, who served for two years before being removed for drunkenness and dishonesty, the court did very little.

2. AR of J. Lee Hall, 1886 (ser. 2467, pp. 345–46).
3. Ibid., p. 349.
4. P. B. Hunt to CIA, Aug. 5, 1878 (OIALR, Roll 383).

Quanah's relation to it, however, had been established and was to continue until January 1898, only three years before the final dissolution of the court.

The outlines of the story of this Comanche, whose judicial career spanned almost the life of his people's court, are familiar. Son of the Comanche chief Peta Nocona and the white captive Cynthia Ann Parker, he was a leader of the several hundred Plains warriors who launched a dawn attack against the buffalo hunters at Adobe Walls, the last great battle the Comanches waged against the white intruders. The last of his people conceded defeat and entered the reservation in 1875. Although the Quahada division of the Comanches to which he belonged had the reputation of being the most dangerous and unruly in the entire tribe, Quanah seems to have decided almost immediately to adjust himself to the new circumstances. Awareness of his white ancestry may have conditioned his response. As he once phrased it: "I am related to both the white and the red people. I realize it is so, and for that reason I will not do anything bad."[5]

Quanah's rise among the Comanches was rapid. Appointed a chief by the agent in 1875, he was but one of about thirty, and his band was not the largest or wealthiest. Cooperation with the agents and military personnel characterized Quanah from the beginning. In 1877 the young chief was dispatched to round up Comanches who had fled the agency in the previous two years. He brought in twenty-one men, women, and children. A year later he turned in to the agent an Indian accused of attempting to murder a soldier at Fort Sill, the military post on the reservation. Fort Sill's commanding officer at this time described Quanah as "the most influential man among the Quahadoz, and one of the most influential

5. Report of General Council at Anadarko, June 10, 1881 (OIALR, 10933, 1881).

among all the bands of the Comanches."[6] It was to the advantage of the whites that he remain so. He had been instructed by the agent to keep an eye on Kiowa medicine making, and in 1887 Quanah warned him that Kiowas had asked the Comanches to join them in an assault on Fort Sill. "Me and my people," Quanah assured the agent, "have quit fighting and we have no desire to join anyone in war again."[7]

Quanah endeared himself to the Texans as well as to the agents and army officers. He used his influence to facilitate leasing of Indian pastures when the cattlemen could no longer avoid some payment. In the heated exchanges that enlivened tribal politics, he was accused of having sold out. Two of the Indians appointed with him to the first court complained through an interpreter to their agents: "We think Qua-nah is bought by the Cattle men and don't come and talk with the rest of us chiefs."[8]

These two chiefs were not on the court when it was reconstituted in 1888. In May of that year Quanah conferred with Special Agent E. E. White, temporarily in charge of the reservation, on a problem which had arisen. Tabatosavit, a fellow tribesman, had shot a Mexican captive of the Comanches and Quanah suggested that perhaps the court should be summoned to handle the matter.[9] White preferred to send the accused to Wichita Falls, where the commissioner ruled the Comanche should be held for trial and, since the Indian was unable to make $500 bail, he was jailed at Dallas.

The agent was aware of the inequity of a system that assigned a Plains warrior to a white man's court for trial for a

6. Lt. Col. J. W. Davidson to Asst. Adj. General, Oct. 29, 1878 (OIALR, Roll 384).

7. Quanah to J. Lee Hall, April 7, 1887 (Quanah Parker File).

8. Tab-a-nan-a-ka and White Wolf to P. B. Hunt, Feb. 5, 1884 (Kiowa LB).

9. Quanah to E. E. White, May 31, 1888 (Quanah Parker File).

crime committed in an Indian community. Ignorant of the law under which he would be tried and the ancient procedures whose origins were obscure even to the white man entangled in their meshes, the Comanche would be truly at the mercy of the court. It was too late to help him, but White decided that revival of the Court of Indian Offenses would mean in the future fewer Tabatosavits in such a fix.

To man the new court White appointed Quanah Parker as presiding judge and Lone Wolf, a Kiowa chief, and Jim Tehuacana of the Wichitas to the other two positions. He proposed salaries of $30 per month for Quanah and $25 for the other two, but the Commissioner of Indian Affairs would approve only $10, more in line with the general salary schedule.[10] In September the court met for the first time and in a case of drunkenness, the only one on the docket, fined the offender $24.[11] This was the only decision in which Lone Wolf shared. The Kiowas objected to their chief serving as a judge and he resigned. His replacement was Chaddle-kaung-ky, Lone Wolf's brother and a policeman.[12]

The Ghost Dance which racked the Sioux reservations in 1890 had relatively little impact on the Kiowa Agency. At the time, the court apparently was not being convened by the agent, and the Kiowas and Comanches were preoccupied with pasture-leasing problems. Quanah also had wife and house trouble, and he had no interest in messiahs. In May 1890 he sent the agent a note, the style of which did no credit to his scribe:

> I hear that the koway and Shianis Say that there are Indian come from heaven and want me to take My People and go to see them But I tell them that I want

10. E. E. White to CIA, July 28, 1888 (Kiowa LB); AR of White, 1888 (ser. 2637, p. 98).

11. Muskogee, *Indian Journal* (Sept. 13, 1888).

12. W. D. Meyers to CIA, Feb. 18, 1889 (Kiowa Court File).

My People to work and pay no attention to that that
we Depend on the Government to help us and no
them.[13]

Both the Kiowas and Comanches were rent with factionalism in the 1890s, and pasture leasing was one of the
principal issues dividing the tribesmen. Not until the spring
of 1892 were legal leases arranged which provided for the
distribution among all the tribesmen of the proceeds from
pasture rent. Prior to this time it appears that some of the
chiefs, Quanah among them, had diverted most of the income to their own pockets. In the summer of 1891 there
were about 100,000 head of cattle grazing the Indian pastures, and an inspector from Washington reported: "Some
of the chiefs and leading men of these tribes are receiving
some money from the cattlemen to keep them quiet, but the
common Indian is not receiving a cent."[14]

Cattlemen who valued his favor possibly contributed to
the building of Quanah's ten-room mansion. He sought
government assistance in its construction and his agent suggested $500 as a reasonable sum, adding: "He is an Indian
who deserves some assistance from the government."[15] Six
years later Quanah was still trying unsuccessfully to obtain
the aid. He insisted that when he brought his band in from
the staked plains to give up their nomadic way of life he
had been promised a house. The Comanche also used the
argument that the Treaty of Medicine Lodge had provided
for the construction of a home for the tribal chief, but all to
no avail. His plurality of wives was a reason advanced for
denying him the financial assistance. Quanah admitted to

13. Quanah to Charles E. Adams, May 13, 1890 (Quanah Parker
File).

14. Arthur W. Tinker to Sec. of the Interior, June 30, 1891 (OIALR,
26273, 1891).

15. Charles E. Adams to CIA, July 18, 1890 (OIALR, 22800, 1890).

more than one wife, but insisted that other Comanches similarly burdened had been helped and that he was being discriminated against. The Commissioner of Indian Affairs was adamant:

> Parker does not deny that he has a plurality of wives, and as it is against the policy of this office to encourage or in anyway countenance polygamy, no assistance will be granted Parker . . . unless he will agree, in writing, to make a choice among his wives and to live only with the one chosen and to fully provide for his other wives, without living with them.[16]

This, Quanah said, he was unable to do as he loved all his wives and children equally. He dropped the problem into the lap of the Commissioner by proposing that the white man make the crucial selection, but there is no evidence that this was done.

The Comanche chief was a curious blend of Conservative and Progressive. In economic matters he was quite cooperative. His relations with the cattlemen were apparently close and mutually profitable. Quanah's name also led the Indian signatures which ratified the Jerome Agreement of 1892. This instrument was negotiated by a team of commissioners led by David Jerome and extended the provisions of the Dawes Severalty Act to the Kiowa and Comanche Reservation. It ultimately led to the allotting of 160 acres of land to each Indian and the sale to whites of excess acreage, over the violent protests of a faction of Kiowas and Comanches. Quanah likewise set an example in acculturation by actually occupying his splendid, star-bedecked house, although he declined to set his hand to the plow. For such menial agricultural duties he employed white farmers.

16. CIA to Charles E. Adams, Sept. 28, 1891 (OIALB, vol. 173).

In other matters he was less of a pleasure to the agents. Quanah used peyote and he refused to support the abolition of Indian dances. Indeed, on one occasion he openly defended peyote and dancing to a group of missionaries.[17] One white investigator condemned these practices as an "aggregation of immorality and indecency."[18] Another, however, dismissed the Ghost Dance at the Kiowa Agency as similar to "camp meetings and revivals among simple-minded and superstitious people of our own race." Nor could the investigator find the "mescal wrecks" supposedly littering the reservation as a result of peyote addiction. He did cite the case of an Indian "dismissed from Carlisle as a hopeless consumptive" who took up peyote "and is today as fine a specimen of health and strength as I could wish to look at." The investigator dismissed Quanah's pigtails as "just double the number affected by George Washington."[19]

Quanah's white blood was not obvious in his physical appearance, but it was frequently alluded to by both whites and Indians. White Wolf, a Comanche of another faction, spoke of him scornfully as a "white man" who "always want to do his own Way."[20] Half-breed and half-blood were other terms applied to Quanah by Indians and whites. But in 1890 his agent could say of him: "He is no white man and has never been treated as such. He is in the office at this moment dressed in buckskin with blanket."[21] A complex personality, usually a Progressive, sometimes a Conservative, he was for thirty-five years a tower of strength to the whites trying to govern his people. Cynthia Parker's son was willing to go

17. G. B. Pray to CIA, Sept. 9, 1898 (OIALR, 41883, 1898).

18. G. B. Pray to CIA, Sept. 12, 1898 (OIALR, 42098, 1898).

19. Report of Investigation of Kiowa Agency, Nov. 30, 1903 (ser. 4646, pp. 468–71).

20. White Wolf to CIA, June 16, 1890 (OIALR, 22798, 1890).

21. Charles E. Adams to CIA, July 17, 1890 (Kiowa LB).

down the white man's road at least part of the way, and he
could command the respect of his fellow tribesmen. These
were qualities essential in an effective policeman or in a
judge of a Court of Indian Offenses.

Despite the meager salary paid to judges, Quanah valued
his position on the court. He had petitioned the agent to
revive the court in 1888, and in 1894 asked that his commission be renewed, although the court was not particularly
active at that time.[22] When one agent set up an arbitration
committee Quanah made certain the Commissioner of Indian Affairs understood that the committee "worked with
and under me, and the Court."[23] Quanah's conduct on the
court was never censured, although that of other judges was.
Agents and inspectors alike agreed that the court performed
a valuable function on the reservation, relieving the agent
of onerous duties and settling disputes which otherwise
would have had to be taken to Texas or Arkansas courts.

A manuscript found among agency papers indicates the
type of case coming before the court and the nature of the
judgments, in not all of which Quanah participated.[24] Nine
meetings of the court are referred to, but on only four occasions were cases tried. The nine cases recorded include two
involving property, three of theft, one of manslaughter, one
of intoxication and assault, and two of marital problems.
The most complicated property case was a contest between
the widow and a brother of a deceased Indian for some
horses, the offspring of a mare owned by the deceased. The
widow, who had been "cast off"—the local form of divorce
—claimed that the mare had been bought with Mexican
blankets which had been traded for eight buffalo robes. The
brother testified to the contrary, that the mare had been pur-

22. Quanah to E. E. White, May 31, 1888 (Quanah Parker File).
23. Quanah to CIA, Sept. 6, 1894 (OIALR, 34227, 1894).
24. Kiowa Court File.

chased with money from the sale of three blacktail deerskins, and the deceased had promised to will him the property. The court ruled for the widow but left no record on the points of law it had found in her favor.

The manslaughter case involved an Indian who had pointed the familiar "unloaded" pistol at a friend with the familiar fatal result. He was found guilty and sentenced to ten days in jail. The drunk, accused of assaulting A'piatan, a nephew of the old chief Lone Wolf, got four days in jail. Guilty verdicts in theft cases resulted in one ten-day sentence and two $10 fines. An Indian found guilty of bigamy was ordered to pay the first, or cast-off wife, a sum of $10 and to present her with a well-broken pony. In the other marital dispute an Indian accused of seducing a wife to desert her husband was found guilty, but given no fine or jail sentence. The woman involved was ordered to return to her husband and remain with him until his other wife, her sister, had recovered from her current illness and, presumably, resumed her wifely duties. Obviously Quanah and his associates were dispensing a brand of justice intelligible to Kiowas and Comanches, but not supportable by the *Federal Reporter.*

It was the marital status of the judges that caused the greatest embarrassment to their agents. The regulations for the court clearly disqualified polygamists. Agent Charles E. Adams wrestled with the problem in the summer and fall of 1890 after the Commissioner had complained of Quanah's several wives. Adams admitted that Quanah had five wives but assured the Commissioner that none had been added to his household that year.[25] In subsequent letters the agent again acknowledged Quanah's plurality of spouses but reaffirmed his other qualifications for the court. "His wives are five undisputed facts," wrote Adams, but, he concluded

25. Charles E. Adams to CIA, Aug. 12, 1890 (Kiowa LB).

optimistically, "I believe he will find his much married position untenable, and will find some way out of his matrimonial entanglements before long." Furthermore, said Adams, "If Quanah is ineligible, any other Comanche who I select would be ineligible for the same reason; the men of influence being, without exception, men of family."[26]

Adams saved Quanah's judgeship that time, but the issue was not dead. It provided a convenient cudgel for those Indians belonging to rival factions on the reservation. Quanah and his chief ally, A'piatan of the Kiowas, led the dominant group. A'piatan was not as forceful as Quanah, but he was quite prominent in his tribe's affairs. He was the leading Kiowa to refuse to sign the Jerome Agreement which provided for the allotment of land in severalty and the ultimate dissolution of the Kiowa–Comanche Reservation. He also had been given the mission of evaluating the messiah Wovoka and his importance to the Kiowas. A'piatan was not impressed by Wovoka, and his negative report undoubtedly helped save the Southern Plains Indians some of the miseries the Ghost Dance brought the Sioux. In the rapidly fluctuating tribal situation he did later become a ghost dancer, just as he altered his views on the Jerome Agreement. But by 1900 he and Quanah were working in close harmony with the agent to implement the Jerome Agreement. In this they were opposed by Ishitti of the Comanches and Lone Wolf and his brother Chaddle-kaung-ky of the Kiowas, who also differed over attorneys to represent the tribe and virtually every other issue that came before the tribes.

Quanah played right into the hands of his enemies by adding to his family obligations. In August 1894 he took to himself his seventh wife and, to compound the error, one claimed by another Indian. For what it was worth, the

26. Ibid., Nov. 3.

woman did indicate a preference for Quanah, and the other
Indian was willing to have his grief assuaged by money and
ponies.[27] But Quanah was not just another Indian violating
the white man's code; he was a judge of the Court of Indian
Offenses and the Principal Chief of the Comanche Tribe.
The incumbent agent, Lieutenant Maury Nichols, a rather
naïve young army officer with little prior experience with
Indians, reported it to Washington. The Commissioner immediately informed Quanah: "This office cannot approve of
such conduct on your part, and unless you will consent to
give this sixth [sic] wife up, it will be necessary . . . to remove
you as a Judge of the Court of Indian Offenses."[28] Under
pressure Quanah signed a pledge which was forwarded to
the Commissioner:

This is to certify that I Quanah Parker principal chief
of the Comanches have this day in compliance with
the wish of the Honorable Commissioner of Indian
Affairs given my word to the act. Indian Agent Lieut.
Maury Nichols 7th U.S. Inf. that I give up and relin-
quish all claims to To-pay, as my wife and will immediately on my return to my home give her back to her
people.[29]

But Quanah then showed up in Washington on tribal
business and returned to inform Lieutenant Nichols that he
had cleared the situation with the Commissioner. And apparently Quanah had found true love; To-pay subsequently
bore him five children, and as her end neared she asked to
be buried by Quanah's side. The other man in the case was

27. George Madera to Lt. Maury Nichols, Aug. 13, 1894 (Quanah
Parker File).
28. CIA to Quanah, Aug. 17, 1894 (OIALB, vol. 286).
29. Quanah's pledge, Aug. 23, 1894 (OIALR, 34170, 1894).

ultimately bought off with a team of horses, a buggy, and $100.[30]

This was the Comanche's last matrimonial venture. Three years later, still a judge on the Court of Indian Offenses, he played a leading role in a reservation council which drew up three new laws on marital relations. They provided for punishment of women deserting their husbands, and of husbands taking up with new women, with or without abandoning the first wife. Plural marriages already contracted were not challenged, thus not disturbing polygamists like Quanah.[31]

The next few months, however, were to bring his troubles to a head. In December, Comanches opposing Quanah met and chose Ishitti to replace Quanah as Principal Chief and Frank Moetah to succeed him on the court. A new Commissioner of Indian Affairs, W. A. Jones, was informed that Quanah and A'piatan were polygamists. He responded with orders to the army officer serving as Indian agent, Captain Frank Baldwin, to remove them from the bench. The Commissioner directed that Chaddle-kaung-ky and Moetah fill the vacancies.[32]

Baldwin defended Quanah and A'piatan, and attacked Chaddle-kaung-ky and Moetah with a heat no civilian would have dared employ. The replacements he denounced as "tricky and deceitful" and "worthless, good-for-nothing," whose appointment "would simply be belittling the dignity of the Court." The incumbents he praised as having "wisely administered justice in every case that has ever been brought before them." He acknowledged that they were polygamists but said it was a matter of long standing. "Both of these

30. George Madera to W. T. Walker, Aug. 14, 1898 (Quanah Parker File).

31. Council Proceedings, July 19–20, 1897 (Kiowa Council File).

32. CIA to Baldwin, Jan. 3, 1898 (Kiowa Court File).

men," insisted Baldwin, "are bitterly opposed to plural marriages and impose a heavy sentence upon anyone who attempts anything of that kind, and for the past three years not a case has occurred that has not been brought before them and has been broken up by their decision." The agent then cited the results of an election conducted when the Indians had collected their payments from pasture leases. As each had approached the table he had been polled, and the result was the election as judges of Quanah, A'piatan, and Apache John. Captain Baldwin denounced the majority of their opponents as "non-progressive Indians, Mexicans and white men with Indian rights, representing the worst element."[33] Baldwin attempted to bypass the Commissioner by asking Captain H. L. Scott, long interested in Kiowa–Comanche affairs, to intercede personally with the Secretary of the Interior and General Nelson A. Miles.[34] In another letter to Commissioner Jones, the agent charged that Jones was "fully under control of that gang of people who have heretofore defrauded and cheated these Indians."[35] But Captain Baldwin's unusually abusive language availed nothing. The Commissioner was firm; Quanah was through as a judge of the Court of Indian Offenses.

Without the services of its most distinguished jurist, the court for the Kiowa Agency limped along for three more years. Captain Baldwin was replaced as agent, and the new man, apparently oblivious of the previous struggle over the judges, nominated A'piatan to succeed Chaddle-kaung-ky, deceased.[36] Indicative of the transitory nature of Washington policy, A'piatan's nomination was approved! Within a few months Kiowas and Comanches of the same factions which

33. Baldwin to CIA, Jan. 8, 1898 (Kiowa LB).
34. Baldwin to Scott, Jan. 10, 1898 (Kiowa LB).
35. Baldwin to CIA, Jan. 11, 1898 *ibid.* (Kiowa LB).
36. James F. Randlett to CIA, May 7, 1900 *ibid.* (Kiowa LB).

had originally unseated Quanah and A'piatan were in Washington complaining that the Kiowa judge was a polygamist. This time the real issue was the pending implementation of the Jerome Agreement, which would result in opening the reservation to white settlement. Quanah and A'piatan were cooperating with the agent, who defended A'piatan in the same terms Baldwin had used earlier to defend Quanah: A'piatan was a polygamist, but also an influential Kiowa whose aid in reservation politics the agent badly needed.[37] But by now the issue had become academic. In the summer of 1901 the reservation was allotted, with the surplus land being sold to white settlers. The Court of Indian Offenses was dissolved.

The court had functioned intermittently for fifteen years. A measure of its importance is the prestige attached to judgeships in the internecine political wars of the reservation. Not only were Kiowas and Comanches like Quanah, A'piatan, Ishitti, and Lone Wolf involved, but also their white attorneys in Washington and Oklahoma, the agents, visiting inspectors, and even the remote Commissioner of Indian Affairs. But as reservations ceased to exist as political and geographical entities, so did the justification for Courts of Indian Offenses.

37. James F. Randlett to CIA, July 6, 1901 (Kiowa Court File).

8. "As Marshals Multiply, Policemen Disappear"

THE DECLINE in importance of Indian courts and Indian police stemmed directly from the impact of the Dawes Act of 1887. It specifically placed the Indian receiving an allotment under the civil and criminal jurisdiction of the state or territory where he resided. Commissioner of Indian Affairs T. J. Morgan reflected this in 1892: "There can . . . be no system of Indian courts where Indians have become citizens of the United States; there can be no system of Indian police."[1] As the tribesmen began to receive their allotments and the citizenship that went with them, and the surplus lands passed into the hands of whites, closed reservations became an anachronism. The tribal courts and police of the Five Civilized Tribes were dealt a death blow by the Curtis Act of 1898, which specifically dissolved their courts and expanded the jurisdiction of federal courts in Indian Territory to "include all causes of action irrespective of the parties."[2] But the courts of these Indians had been diminishing in importance for several years as new federal courts had

1. Report of the Board of Indian Commissioners, 1892 (ser. 3088, p. 1303).
2. AR of W. A. Jones, 1898 (ser. 3757, p. 75). The Curtis Act applied the allotment principle of the Dawes Severalty Act to the Five Civilized Tribes and provided for dissolution of their governments by 1906.

been established or the jurisdiction of courts in nearby states expanded.

"As marshals multiply, policemen disappear," declared the head of the Union Agency, "and yet while this agency remains intact there must be some medium through which its orders can be executed and its powers asserted."[3] This was the common experience of agents. The paramilitary character of the Sioux Reservation forces faded as it became apparent that the tribesmen had lost the capacity to resist. There still remained, however, a need for police. A Nez Percé agent wanted to retain at least one officer to identify members of the tribe for determining heirs and making up payrolls. Others spoke of their usefulness as reservation handymen. Navajo policemen were still employed as trackers as late as the 1920s, when one Be-gay was commended for following a trail that crossed beds of pine needles and outcroppings of rock. Not even the fugitive's stratagem of driving a herd of horses before him and changing mounts without touching the ground deflected Be-gay.[4] But duties of this nature did not require forces of thirty or forty men and, while the number of agencies with police did not decline appreciably, the total number of policemen did. The average reservation now had only one or two, and in 1927 even the largest Sioux force consisted of only seventeen men.[5] No longer did army officers on detached duty as agents thrill to the sight of mounted Indian police units galloping through intricate cavalry drills under the watchful eye of old sergeants.

More of the reservations lost their Indian courts than lost their police forces and, where the courts remained, their

3. AR of Dew M. Wisdom, 1897 (ser. 3641, p. 139).

4. Albert H. Kneale, *Indian Agent* (Caldwell, 1950), p. 367.

5. Laurence F. Schmeckebier, *The Office of Indian Affairs* (Baltimore, 1927), p. 356.

character gradually changed. Increasingly they served merely to record vital statistics or provide preliminary hearings to determine which tribal difficulties were to be carried before off-reservation courts. Minor cases might come before them, but their function seemed to be more to conciliate or arbitrate than to determine legality. Where they did retain the character of courts, their procedures continued to have a breezy informality not found in American courts since Colonial times. In the 1920s Secretary of the Interior Hubert Work reported that in some Indian courts unsworn witnesses testified, a prisoner charged with one crime would be convicted of another, rules of evidence were unknown, and, "No offender escapes . . . because of any technicality."[6]

The dissolution of a reservation and the sudden demise of its Indian court sometimes resulted in chaos. The allotted Indian manifested his lack of preparation for his new status by seeing only the privileges, not the responsibilities, of his new status. As the Tulalip Agent observed sardonically: "The Indian is quick . . . to avail himself of one of the inalienable rights of American citizenship, and gets gloriously drunk, having no dread of punishment by Indian courts or agent."[7]

All sorts of complications arose as jurisdiction presumably shifted to local law enforcement agencies and courts. The sale of surplus land to whites eliminated the clear line which had delineated the reservation from the white communities grown up around it. A common development was for the county and state authorities either to declare they had no jurisdiction or to ignore the matter because of the expense of servicing Indian communities that paid no tax. In one curious situation in Washington Territory, judges of the Indian court petitioned to lower the fine on drunkenness in

6. Secretary of the Interior Hubert Work, "The Indian Courts" (Records of the Board of Indian Commissioners, Tray 109).

7. AR of D. C. Govan, 1895 (ser. 3382, p. 318).

order to be competitive with courts of neighboring towns which were levying smaller fines than the Indian courts. And, the agent warned, "They being all citizens, it may be a question whether or not the regulation could be enforced if put to a test, and to have a case of that kind would be very bad for the court."[8]

Honest disagreement over areas of jurisdiction did exist. Despite Commissioner Morgan's dictum that Indian citizenship removed the basis for Indian courts, around the turn of the century a few additional courts were being established or defunct ones revived. The Indians at the Umatilla Agency importuned their administrator to seek permission from Washington to reopen theirs. "Its reestablishment," he later announced, "has been hailed with joy by the better class of Indians, as it is an unheard of occurrence for an Indian to prosecute another Indian in civil courts, where they have to employ lawyers and pay cutthroat fees."[9]

The occasional new or revived court, and the ones that persisted, were not universally acclaimed. More than one tribesman summoned before a Court of Indian Offenses now charged that as an allotted Indian he was no longer under the jurisdiction of such a court. Still, when Yellow Bull and Clarence Running-After-Arrow were hailed into the Ponca Agency's court for drunkenness, and protested its authority over citizens, the incumbent Secretary of the Interior held that even if allotment had taken place the Indians were still subject to government control if they lived within the boundaries of the reservation.[10] Some justification for the Secretary's ruling is to be found in the fact that allotted Indians did not receive a clear title to their land for twenty-five years. Thus, even though citizenship presumably accompanied al-

8. E. Eels to CIA, July 26, 1887 (OIALR, 20287, 1887).
9. George W. Harper to CIA, March 5, 1897 (OIALR, 9531, 1887).
10. Sec. of the Interior to CIA, Nov. 5, 1903 (OIALR, 71691, 1903).

lotment, the Indian whose land was still in trust might be, for some purposes, a minor in the eyes of the law.

These jurisdictional ambiguities had haunted the Indian police and courts from their inception, and were typical of the confused legal status of the Indian. It had taken two murders in 1881 to finally bring that crime on reservations under the jurisdiction of federal courts. At Pine Ridge, Spotted Elk shot down White Cow Walking; Rosebud was the scene of the murder, already recounted, of the famed Spotted Tail by Crow Dog. Both Crow Dog and Spotted Elk were arrested and taken to Deadwood for trial. Crow Dog was tried first, found guilty, and sentenced to be hanged. On appeal, he was freed by the Supreme Court, which found that there was no law against an Indian killing an Indian on a reservation.[11] Within fifteen months a shocked Congress had acted. Brushing aside proposals to extend all federal criminal and civil jurisdiction over the Indians, and excepting the Five Civilized Tribes, it did define seven acts committed by Indians on reservations as federal crimes: murder, manslaughter, rape, assault with intent to kill, arson, burglary, and larceny. Congress expanded the list in 1909 and 1932 to include incest, assault with a dangerous weapon, and robbery. In 1956 another offense was added to the "Ten Major Crimes"—this one designed to cover embezzlement by tribal officials.[12]

No such federal legislation had defined the jurisdiction of the Courts of Indian Offenses, and the courts and the police were constantly being challenged. The usual reaction of the Commissioners of Indian Affairs was to try to avoid a showdown. As an example we have the case of a Santee Sioux who brought an infidelity charge against his wife and wanted

11. *Ex Parte Crow Dog* (109 U.S. 556).
12. Laurence Davis, "Criminal Jurisdiction over Indian Country in Arizona," *Arizona Law Review* (Spring 1959), p. 76.

the matter tried in the Court of Indian Offenses. His wife
and the agent insisted upon a state court, since the Santee
Reservation had been allotted and the Indians were now
taxpayers. The word from Washington was that the Court
of Indian Offenses should be inactivated as it was now an
unnecessary expense and it might also lead to an Indian's
being tried in two courts on the same charge and raise questions about the legality of the Indian courts.[13] Likewise,
when the Nez Percé agent inquired whether to inactivate
his police force and court, the reply was similar: continue
them unless some conflict develops with local authorities.[14]
And when, in a case previously mentioned, a Washington
state court awarded Hoot-et-soot $25 damages for false
imprisonment and a forced haircut by the Umatilla court and
police, the Commissioner of Indian Affairs advised the Secretary of the Interior not to appeal it.[15]

The presence on reservations of white squatters, squaw-
men, and mixed-bloods produced another type of jurisdictional problem. In 1895 one arose in Nebraska. The agent
was using police to evict whites who had leased land from
the Flournoy Live Stock and Real Estate Company for 25
cents to $2.50 an acre. The company in turn had leased the
land from the Indians at a top of 50 cents per acre, and it
first tried to stop the agent by injunctions. Then a local
sheriff tried to arrest an Indian policeman, only to be arrested himself and brought before the agent. The agent
promptly swore out a warrant against the sheriff before a
justice of the peace, and the sheriff prepared to organize a
posse to arrest the agent. The latter asked and got an increase
in the size of his reservation force and the shipment of
seventy Springfield rifles from the War Department. Open

13. CIA to Sec. of the Interior, March 8, 1890 (OIALB, vol. 195).
14. CIA to D. M. Browning, Sept. 24, 1895 (OIALB, vol. 315).
15. CIA to Sec. of the Interior, Feb. 14, 1896 (OIALR, 5441, 1896).

warfare appeared imminent as evictions by the police were halted by an injunction the lessees obtained from a federal judge. A compromise was finally worked out, through the intercession of Nebraska congressmen, by which the lessees would be permitted to remain long enough to harvest crops.[16]

In another case involving jurisdiction of Indian police over whites, William Fielder, a squaw man at the Cheyenne River Agency, attempted to kill his wife. When seven Indian police tried to arrest him, Fielder seized an ax and a policeman killed him in self-defense. All seven were tried for murder at Deadwood and two were found guilty of assault with intent to do bodily harm. Their sentences were later set aside, but the litigation cost the policemen over $2,000. As word of the incident spread through the Sioux agencies, their police considered resigning in a body to protest what they considered harassment.[17]

The mixed-blood question was even more awkward. A federal judge in South Dakota ruled that mixed-blood Indians were not Indians as defined by federal law and therefore not triable in United States courts.[18] This then raised the question, which still exists, of how to persuade state courts to take jurisdiction when Indian communities do not produce sufficient tax revenues to pay for such services.

Finally, there was the issue of Indian policeman making arrests off the reservation. American Horse and Big Knee, police at the Cheyenne and Arapaho Agency, arrested a drunken Indian on his own allotment and threw him into the agency jail. Sobering up overnight, the indignant citizen went to a nearby town and swore out a warrant for the arrest

16. AR of D. M. Browning, 1895 (ser. 3382, pp. 39–41).

17. AR of Peter Couchman, 1895 (ser. 3382, p. 283); Leupp, *The Indian and His Problem,* p. 244.

18. AR of Chas. E. McChesney, 1899 (ser. 3915, pp. 341–42).

of the two policemen, but a justice of the peace cleared them.[19]

A comparable dilemma arose in Oregon when a state judge served a writ of habeas corpus on Old Wolf, the Umatilla Agency jailer, for prisoners No Shirt and Young Chief. The two had been imprisoned by order of the Court of Indian Offenses for resisting Indian police, but the judge held that neither the Indian court nor the police had any authority over No Shirt and Young Chief, since they had taken their allotments.[20]

Usually when the right of the police or the courts was challenged, the Commissioner of Indian Affairs reacted as he did when apprised of the killing of a policeman who was making an arrest off reservation: "I do not think it would be wise to bring the right of the police to make arrests in such cases into question before the Courts, lest it should result in the denial of such tacit consent hereafter."[21]

In dubious cases involving off-reservation arrests by Indian police, the caution of the Bureau of Indian Affairs is understandable. It had, however, received favorable rulings on the courts and police. In *United States* v. *Clapox* (35 Fed. 575), a federal judge in Oregon in 1888 had sustained, beyond question, the right of the United States to create Courts of Indian Offenses and reservation police forces. The case had originated with the arrest by Indian police and the proposed trial, by the Umatilla court, of Minnie, an Indian woman charged with immoral behavior. While still awaiting trial she was rescued from the agency jail by the present defendants. Although the judge agreed that the Courts of Indian Offenses were not part of the system authorized by the Constitution, indeed, were "mere educational and disciplin-

19. AR of Charles F. Ashley, 1892 (ser. 3088, p. 372).
20. Geo. W. Harper to CIA, March 13, 1895 (OIALR, 12268, 1895).
21. CIA to Daniel W. Matthews, April 5, 1892 (OIALB, vol. 234).

ary instrumentalities," the judge ruled against the rescuers. As he saw it, the United States was in effect the "guardian" of the Indians, and the reservation was a "school" where the Indians might acquire "the habits, ideas, and aspirations which distinguish the civilized from the uncivilized man." Adultery being clearly an immoral and undesirable practice, the United States in its capacity as guardian could ban it and provide machinery for "the arrest, trial, and punishment of any Indian guilty of a violation of the same." This decision provided the precedent cited in every subsequent ruling upholding the legality of reservation police forces and Courts of Indian Offenses. It was backed by an earlier decision, *United States* v. *Kagama* (118 U.S. 375) clarifying the power of a federal court, under the Seven Crimes Act, to try Kagama for murdering a fellow Indian on a reservation. "These Indians *are* the wards of the nation," said the court. "They are communities *dependent* on the United States."

As hope faded that the time was imminent when Indians would be totally absorbed into American society, Courts of Indian Offenses and Indian police became fixtures in Indian communities. The judges and police continued to perform valuable services for small compensation. In 1938 at least one Washington official returned from a tour of inspection convinced the police were a real bargain. On being asked by the official to describe in detail what he had done for a month to merit his $45 salary and the two sacks of oats he received for his horse, a policeman's recital had been impressive. He reported that in the first ten days he had spent sixty-eight hours in the saddle trailing three men who had killed a steer; twenty-two hours were expended in eliminating a rabid coyote. Then followed a four-day assignment to take a sick Indian over a hundred miles of trail to a hospital. An estimated 112 hours were used in gathering evidence on cattle thieves. "But I ain't counted my night work yet,"

continued the policeman. This included twenty calls to keep
order at Indian dances and ninety-seven hours consumed in
breaking up fights. And all this for $45 and two sacks of
oats![22] Obviously a policeman's lot had not improved measurably since the day of Sam Sixkiller.

Even the legislation in 1924 granting citizenship to all
Indians did not disturb the courts and the police. By the
late 1920s another wave of reform was beginning to build
up as public indignation was aroused by reports of new raids
on Indian land and of the degraded conditions of the native
Americans in a generally prosperous United States. The
Meriam Report on the problem of Indian administration,
instigated by Secretary of the Interior Hubert Work and
published in 1928, made no sweeping recommendations on
the subjects of law and justice. The authors of the report
found the situations varied too greatly from tribe to tribe.[23]

The problem of reservation law and order was undergoing re-examination by others. Four options were being
considered: turn the entire problem over to state courts;
provide a special federal code; employ tribal courts on some
reservations; enforce state laws in federal courts.[24] The
Board of Indian Commissioners' suggestion was to extend
state law to the reservations where the Secretary of the Interior believed the Indians were sufficiently acculturated.[25]

The Wheeler-Howard Indian Reorganization Act of 1934

22. "One Indian Lawman," in *Indians at Work* (Oct. 1939), p. 11.

23. Under the direction of Dr. Lewis Meriam and financed by a grant
from John D. Rockefeller, Jr., specialists in fields including law, education, and health visited Indian communities throughout the United
States. Their report gave priority to medical and school improvements
and the creation of a long-range planning division. The report also
recommended raising personnel standards in the Indian Service and a
much closer scrutiny of proposals for further allotment.

24. AR of the Sec. of the Interior, 1932, p. 47.

25. Ibid., 1930, p. 52.

was the culmination of the reform movement initiated in the 1920s.[26] One of the sweeping changes it was to have accomplished was in the area of law and order. In the process of passage through Congress, however, the title providing a special court of Indian affairs was dropped. But new regulations for law and order did improve the functioning of existing Indian courts and, with the organization of tribal governments under the Wheeler-Howard Act came a new type of tribunal. Although the name might vary from reservation to reservation, the new institutions were termed collectively "tribal courts." By 1964 there were fifty-one of them in operation, in contrast with only eleven Courts of Indian Offenses.[27]

The new tribal courts could administer the same Department of Interior regulations that had been the province of the Courts of Indian Offenses, or they might dispense justice in terms of a code drawn up by the particular tribe and approved by the Secretary of the Interior. But regardless of which code was administered, the same problems of jurisdiction plagued these courts as had plagued their predecessors in the late nineteenth century.

The most frequently cited current example of regulation of tribal law and order, although it is in no way typical, is that of the Navajos. The sheer size and complexity of it are impressive. The Navajos budget over a million dollars a year for maintenance of their police and court systems for 85,000 people. A Navajo trial court, staffed by seven judges,

26. The act gave a new direction to Indian policy. It did not force change on the tribes but rather permitted them to take advantage of the terms if they so desired. Tribes might now rule themselves under their own constitutions, allotment acts were repealed, and credits were made available for Indian agricultural and industrial projects, to cite only some of the act's outstanding provisions.

27. Deputy Assistant Commissioner of Indian Affairs William E. Finale to the author, May 18, 1964.

handles cases which prior to 1959 would have been tried before Courts of Indian Offenses. The final authority is not the Secretary of the Interior but the Court of Appeals of the Navajo Tribe. The Indians also have taken over complete responsibility for policing their reservation. And their equipment includes all the modern paraphernalia of law enforcement; these Indian police carry six-shooters, but they ride radio-equipped patrol cars, not paint ponies.

The Navajo courts differ considerably from the state and federal courts in Arizona. In the absence of trained personnel —as late as 1959 only one Navajo was a lawyer[28]—they retain much of the informality of the old Courts of Indian Offenses. Because about half the adults of the tribe do not speak English, court proceedings more likely than not are conducted in Navajo.

Nor until 1965 was there any relief in the United States Constitution for an Indian or white who felt his rights had been infringed upon in any Navajo or other tribal court. In 1896 in *Talton* v. *Mayes* (163 U.S. 376) the Supreme Court had ruled that the United States statutes and the provisions of the Constitution that regulate normal court operation had no validity relative to Indian courts. But in 1965 a federal district court in Montana ruled, in a case involving a Gros Ventre, Madeline Colliflower, that Indian courts are in part "arms of the Federal Government."[29] A lower court, to which the case had been returned, then ruled that there had been a lack of due process under the Fifth Amendment.[30] This would seem to indicate that in the future Indian courts will be held accountable to the same standards which prevail for other courts. The system con-

28. Laurence Davis, "Court Reform in the Navajo Nation," *Journal of the American Judicature Society* (Aug. 1959), p. 53.

29. New York *Times* (March 28, 1965), p. 48.

30. *Time* (Sept. 3, 1965), p. 72.

ceived in the nineteenth century will be brought into line with the modern concepts of the rights of the accused, thereby eliminating one of the most objectionable features of Indian courts.

9. "They Are Not Perfect, But . . . "

ANY EVALUATION of the Indian police and judges must take into consideration the objectives of their originators. Although the virtue of extending a system of laws over the Indians had been discussed for many years, both police and courts seem to have been reactions to immediate problems. In the field in the 1870s, the John Clums were clamoring for help in administering their agencies, and both agents and officials in Washington were anxious for an alternative to reliance on the military. The police were the answer. The experiment was launched on a shoestring, as the pitiful salaries and initial absence of uniforms and weapons indicated.

Two years after the first police force appeared, Commissioner of Indian Affairs E. M. Marble, citing a poll of the agents, declared them an unqualified success. He stated that what "was at first undertaken as an experiment, is now looked upon as a necessity."[1] Schurz also noted a fringe benefit that would become one of the principal rationalizations for both police and judges: the police expedited the acculturation process by diminishing the authority of the chiefs and discouraging traditional practices deemed uncivilized by the agents. This would lead, it was hoped, to the ultimate dissolution of the tribe and the absorption of its members into the mainstream of American society.

1. AR of Sec. of the Interior Carl Schurz, 1880 (ser. 1959, p. 10).

In 1892 Commissioner T. J. Morgan maintained that the Courts of Indian Offenses, as well as the police, were established "for the purpose of relieving the anomalous conditions that existed on Indian reservations by reason of an absence of laws applicable to Indians."[2] There had certainly been need for some tribunal before which reservation malefactors might be brought by Indian police. Nevertheless, the Courts of Indian Offenses originated not in this need but in Secretary Teller's abhorrence of certain Indian sexual and religious customs. The courts had had an even shakier beginning than the police, and five years passed before Congress appropriated money to pay judges, thus endowing them with at least a shadow of legality.

With some pride of authorship, Teller, back in the Senate in 1899, remarked: "There was only one opinion regarding the courts that I ever heard of, and that was that they were a desirable aid in keeping peace and order on the reservations."[3] And this was the general sentiment of the personnel of the Indian Service. The agent who now had a police force to back his orders and supplement his work force, and a tribal court to relieve him of a perplexing and unpopular role, did endorse them. The degree of enthusiasm of his commendation varied in direct proportion to his ability to inspire loyalty and efficiency among his police and judges. A

2. AR of Morgan, 1892 (ser. 3088, p. 25).

3. *Congressional Record,* 32(1)(1898), 650. Teller had not wavered in his support of the police and courts. In a debate on the Indian appropriation bill in 1890 he said: "I do not believe it possible to maintain order on the reservations without the police, and I do not believe that in the whole bill there is any money that is to be better expended than that expended for Indian police and the Indian courts." He was supported by his colleague Gideon C. Moody of South Dakota: "There is no plan that has ever been devised or used that is so well calculated to preserve peace upon those agencies as this plan of appointment of policemen and of police magistrates." *Congressional Record,* 21(8)(1890), 7603–05.

few agents concluded that the tribal character of their charges ruled out any possibility that either institution would work well on their reservations. But more typical were the reactions of agents administering the Standing Rock and Quapaw reservations. From Dakota Territory the first agent reported his police a "terror to the evil doers, both white and Indian."[4] The Quapaw agent in Indian Territory saw the same quality: "perfect ferrets after criminals," he dubbed his police. His comment: "They are not perfect, but we could not get along without them at all," is probably the best summary of the agents' evaluation of the police.[5]

The courts inspired comparable opinions, as witness a memorandum by Secretary of the Interior Hubert Work some forty years after their establishment:

> That these Indian courts have worked admirably and have proved of educational value to the Indians, there is little doubt. They have taught the Indian respect for the law. They have acquainted them with American jurisprudence. They have served to train them in the duties of good citizenship. . . . Needless to relate, the Indian courts are not successful on all reservations.[6]

The most sweeping indictment of either judges or police by a member of the Indian Service was made by Special Agent H. Heth, who invoked his record of forty years among the Indians to strengthen the credibility of his statement. "I wish no better evidence of an Indian Agent's incapacity or worthlessness," Heth wrote the Indian Commissioner, "than when I read in his annual report, that he is saved much trouble by his Indian Judges." Heth was con-

4. AR of J. A. Stephan, 1881 (ser. 2018, p. 117).
5. AR of D. B. Dyer, 1882 (ser. 2100, p. 145).
6. Sec. Work, "The Indian Courts" (MS).

vinced that the judges would not punish anyone "rich, influential, or a friend."[7]

While this special agent's attitude was unusual among Indian Service personnel, criticism of the judges and police was common among self-styled friends of the Indian. They were not a numerous group but quite vocal and capable of embarrassing any administration in Washington which dared ignore them. Their man in the Senate was Henry L. Dawes of Massachusetts, and they were represented on the Board of Indian Commissioners which scrutinized expenditures of the Indian Bureau and offered gratuitous advice on handling the red men. By coincidence, the same year (1883) that the Courts of Indian Offenses were inaugurated, the reformers gathered for the first meeting of the Lake Mohonk Conference. This annual outing at a hotel owned by the Quaker Albert K. Smiley would become the principal sounding board for the friends of the Indian and their opportunity to reach a consensus on policies to recommend to the government.

Whether expressed in the forum provided at Lake Mohonk, on the floor of Congress, in the minutes of the Board of Indian Commissioners, in resolutions of the American Bar Association, or in articles in periodicals, the burden of the reformers was apparent. They were most unhappy about the continued lack of a system of law for the reservations and the power this left in the hands of the agents. As the Indians' own systems of social control had deteriorated in the presence of the new conditions reservation life presented, the agent had ceased to be just the official contact between the United States and tribal chieftains. Now he often was civil administrator, police chief, judge, and jury—the source of all authority for several thousand people scattered over hun-

7. Heth to CIA, April 22, 1889 (OIALR, 11642, 1889).

dreds of square miles. Reformers attacking the system called it "evil,"[8] damned the agent as "a little king,"[9] and stigmatized the agency as an "autocracy,"[10] "a little Russia."[11]

The problem was how to bring the Indian under state and territorial law before he became a taxpayer. Immediate citizenship was a panacea some urged. But one critic of this equated the introduction of the Indian into our political life with the influx of "adventurers of every land—the Communists of France, the Socialists of Germany, the Nihlists of Russia, and the cut-throat murderers of Ireland." He predicted it would demoralize the Indians, who were completely unprepared for such power. He reminded his readers that the Declaration of Independence characterized the Indians as "merciless savages," and he dismissed them as "the only native sporting class in America."[12]

Such fears of Indian bloc voting were baseless. It was discovered after the Dawes Severalty Act went into effect that citizenship and an allotment of land did not necessarily bring the Indian access to the ballot box and an accepted place in white society. As the reformers groped for a policy on law to cover the transition period, their views of the Indian police and Courts of Indian Offenses were clarified. There was less comment about the police, and most of that favorable. In 1891 Senator Dawes referred to them during debate over appropriations for Indian affairs as the "bulwark

8. James B. Thayer, in Proceedings of the Lake Mohonk Conference, 1888 (ser. 2637, p. 801).

9. Rev. Thomas L. Riggs, in Proceedings of the Lake Mohonk Conference, 1890 (ser. 2841, p. 854).

10. Report of the Board of Indian Commissioners, 1892 (ser. 2934, p. 1102).

11. Elaine Goodale, "Plain Words on the Indian Question," *New England Magazine* (April 1890), p. 147.

12. G. M. Lamberton, "Indian Citizenship," *American Law Review,* 20 (1886), 187–88.

of the Government in the administration of justice and in the preservation of order on the reservation."[13] He said the police experiment had done more than anything except the severalty law to elevate the Indian. Coming from Henry L. Dawes, this was high praise indeed! There was criticism of the police for reinforcing the agent's autocracy, but as late as 1906 the Board of Indian Commissioners judged them "indispensable if law and order are to prevail upon the reservations."[14]

The Courts of Indian Offenses earned few such encomiums. The power of the agent to appoint the judges and overrule their decisions disturbed many observers. Bishop W. D. Walker of Dakota Territory di ' defend the courts before a Lake Mohonk audience, citing one he had observed functioning with a dignity equal to that of a New York police court.[15] But the usual comment was less laudatory, although the crities admitted that the courts performed a needed function.

The hope that regular courts, administering either federal and state law or a special code, would replace the Indian courts, only gradually faded with the demise of the Thayer Bill,[16] which was introduced into the Senate in 1888 by

13. Report of the Board of Indian Commissioners, 1892 (ser. 2934, p. 1168).

14. Ibid., 1906 (ser. 4960, p. 7).

15. Proceedings of the Lake Mohonk Conference, 1890 (ser. 2841, p. 855).

16. In 1885 the Board of Indian Commissioners expressed hostility to a special code and special courts: "But, aside from the great expense of such a system, it is open to the objection that it would perpetuate the evil that has grown out of our treaty and reservation policy of keeping the Indians apart from all others, and of maintaining a hundred petty sovereignties within our borders. We believe that the laws which are good enough for all other kindreds and peoples and tribes and nations are good enough for Indians." Proceedings of the Board of Indian Commissioners, 1885 (ser. 2287, p. 684).

Dawes. The bill would have provided a special code and special courts for reservations. Despite backing from the Indian Rights Association, the Boston Indian Citizenship Committee, and the Connecticut and Massachusetts Indian Association, the bill never got out of committee. Senator Dawes himself was dubious of its constitutionality and considered that it made elaborate and expensive provisions for a situation he judged ephemeral. By 1891 Professor Thayer had lost hope that the bill carrying his name would ever be enacted, although he felt there still existed a necessity to extend a system of "real courts and real law" to the reservations. Thayer acknowledged that the Courts of Indian Offenses had had a "salutary and steadying effect," but compared them to courts-martial, "really a branch of the executive department." The Indian judges, he noted, "do not administer law, but merely certain rules of the Indian Department."[17] For Americans as yet unfamiliar with federal agencies administering their own sets of regulations in a quasi-judicial fashion, Thayer's criticism was a serious one.

But Thayer did give the Indian courts high marks for their educational function, as did others. *The Independent* carried an editorial in 1902 which summarized this attitude. The writer pronounced the courts "primary schools of law" where the Indian judges "have been learning and teaching the a b c of legal procedure." He believed they frequently had been "a real power making for righteousness."[18] Yet the

17. Thayer, "A People Without Law," *Atlantic Monthly* (Nov. 1891), p. 683. On another occasion, at a Lake Mohonk Conference, Thayer summarized his view of the legal position of the Indian: "If they are not a separate people, to be dealt with by treaty, then they are a subject people, to be fully legislated for and to be absorbed. They must come in out of the rain under the cover of our Constitution with the rest of us." Proceedings of the Lake Mohonk Conference, 1888 (ser. 2637, p. 799).

18. "The Lawless Indian," *The Independent* (March 5, 1903), p. 576.

writer, like so many others, was concerned about the Indians who had become citizens but were still not provided for in state and territorial law. He exhibited very little curiosity about the reaction of the individual Indian to the legal experiments imposed on him, making the customary assumption of the white man that any evidence of abandonment of native ways constituted progress.

"The life of law has not been logic: it has been experience," Justice Oliver Wendell Holmes was saying, but few applied this dictum to the spectacle of white Americans imposing their concepts of justice on red Americans. If there had been a single Indian culture, instead of a bewildering multitude of apparently infinite variety, conceivably the native law-ways would have been treated with more respect. Or had the native Americans been concentrated, instead of scattered among a much larger and rapidly growing white population, it would have been easier and more logical to take their culture into account in formulating their legal codes. With the exception of one small reform faction headed by T. A. Bland, however, reformers and Indian Service personnel were united in the conviction that the native cultures had lost their vigor, and whatever value they might once have had for the Indian was rapidly disappearing.

It is much easier to determine the views of whites on the Indian police and judges than to speculate on how the tribesmen reacted when the institutions were installed on the reservations. Compared to other government policies, the provisions for judges and police, particularly the latter, did seem an extension of tribal institutions. Soldier societies had performed police functions; chiefs and headmen had arbitrated intratribal disputes. Only a recognition of this basis in the old culture can explain the influence the Indian police and judges did enjoy.

Other things, of course, contributed to their greater success on particular reservations. The policeman's position appears to have been more satisfying to him at the larger agencies, which had forces organized along military lines. The training he received and the feeling of being a member of a unit, which he derived from living in a police barracks instead of being the lone representative of an alien power in one of the widely scattered Indian camps, obviously contributed to a policeman's morale.

The agent's ability to select the proper personnel as judges and police was the principal key to the success of the programs. But what could persuade an Indian to align himself with the agent, and, frequently, against his tribal elders and the traditions of his people? Probably it was the power and prestige the positions carried. For a people among whom the fighting tradition was still strong, the uniforms of the police, their right to bear arms among warriors now weaponless, and the scouting missions they conducted against renegades would have been strong attractions. As policemen they visited all corners of the reservation and were the embodiment of the extratribal power that was growing yearly. The Indian policeman even commanded the grudging respect of white men residing on or visiting the reservation. An opportunity to exercise power, command such respect, and evoke some relationship with a warrior past would go a long way toward compensating for the inadequate pay and the jeers, tinged with fear and envy, of one's fellow tribesmen.

A position on the bench of the agency's Court of Indian Offenses carried power of even more impressive dimensions. The policeman might arrest the culprit, but the justices weighed the evidence and pronounced judgment. Operating near the center of the agency's power structure, the judge not only shared in it by virtue of his position but acquired a knowledge of agency administrative procedures and American law and customs, and established a personal relationship with those who now directed his people's destiny. A Sitting Bull might sulk in his cabin while his influence and prestige waned with his prowess as a medicine man and warrior. Younger, more flexible men, like Quanah, recognized where the power now lay and maneuvered to grasp it. It was certainly not the pay that made a position on the Kiowa–Comanche court such a prize in the intratribal politicking.

A seat on the bench, or a badge, did not bring with it an automatic shift of loyalties. The old ties were strong and the new status difficult to understand. The Indian now was expected to cleave to an impersonal state, whereas his loyalties to his relatives and fellow tribesmen had always been much more personal. Orders to arrest a relative, or the necessity of passing judgment on a fellow clansman, created conflicts— the undoing of many a policeman or judge. Also, the old religious beliefs persisted, and some shamans successfully challenged the new order, badges and commissions paling in significance before their medicine.

The most effective police and judges of the late nineteenth century had a foot in each camp. Quanah was not a white man, as his agents pointed out. He might aspire to wealth and political power in terms any white man could comprehend, but Quanah was also a bulwark of the peyote cult. The Sioux George Sword has left us a record of his dilemma. A war leader and medicine man before he became Captain of United States Indian Police at Pine Ridge, he had scars on his chest to prove he had participated in the Sun Dance. Although Sword had forsaken this most pervasive ceremonial of the Plains Indian, and had become a deacon in a Christian church, he still feared to offend his Indian gods. Sword's explanation—"because the spirit of an Oglala may go to the spirit land of the Lakota"—must have represented

the type of hedging engaged in by many Sioux of his generation.[19] The white man's medicine appeared to have proved
its superiority in combat, but . . .

It was around 1915 that Sword expressed his doubts, so it
should not be surprising that a quarter century earlier there
should have been many Indians who were as yet unable to
grasp the new legal concepts. A particularly dramatic example of this was acted out in 1890 at the Tongue River
Agency in Montana. The principal roles were played by two
young Northern Cheyennes, Head Chief and Young Mule.

The Northern Cheyennes, about a thousand strong, had
been located on the Tongue and Rosebud rivers since 1881.
Hostile during the Sioux War of 1876, by 1890 they had
been forced by circumstances to give up their nomadic life.
Buffalo had grazed the valleys of the Tongue and Rosebud
when the Cheyennes located there, but by 1890 they had
disappeared, and the Indians, showing little inclination to
turn to agriculture, were subsisting on government rations.

Their agents had set up a police force and an Indian court,
but the latter was not established until 1889, and the police
were undependable. Captain of Police at the time of the 1890
difficulty was White Hawk, although subsequently he was
discharged for a lack of enthusiasm in returning truants to
school. White Hawk then turned to religion and persuaded
some of the Northern Cheyennes that he had discovered
a new messiah who would resurrect the dead Indians, re-
placing them under a nearby mountain with the whites. This
defines the quality of the police at Tongue River and indicates how little affected were the Northern Cheyennes by a
decade of reservation life.

Coinciding with the tribe's flirtation with the messiah

19. J. R. Walker, "The Sun Dance and Other Ceremonies of the
Oglala Division of the Teton Dakota," in Clark Wissler, ed., *Sun
Dance of the Plains Indians* (New York, 1921), p. 159.

movement was trouble stemming from the intrusions of cattlemen into Cheyenne land: Indians killed an occasional steer; the cattlemen heard rumors of a new inflammatory Indian religion and demanded protection; troops were brought in. Then in May 1890 a cowboy was found murdered, and there were predictions of a war between the cattlemen and the Cheyennes. This crisis was safely passed, but in September young Hugh Boyle, recently arrived from the East to visit relatives, was found shot through the head and clubbed. Special Agent James A. Cooper, temporarily assigned to Tongue River, learned from Chief American Horse that the murderers were Head Chief and Young Mule, youths about the age of their victim.

Agent Cooper called the Cheyennes into council and demanded the murderers. After conferring, the Indians offered to pay thirty ponies for the killing. This was good Indian practice but completely unacceptable to the white man. Insisting that the letter of the law be obeyed, Cooper again demanded the persons of Head Chief and Young Mule. Unable to buy their way out of their difficulty with ponies, and unwilling to surrender themselves to trial, Head Chief and Young Mule chose to expiate their crime by dying in battle against the white troopers. The father of one of them delivered their message: "Select the place of meeting and we will come to die in your sight." This was hardly trial by combat, for the outcome was certain; it smacked more of a gladiatorial spectacle. The agent protested, but the Indians were adamant. The father returned to Head Chief and Young Mule to inform them of the verdict and help them paint and array themselves and their horses for the finale.

By the middle of the afternoon the stage was set in the valley in which the agency headquarters was located. One troop of cavalry and some Indian police were drawn up on a road running through the valley; another troop had taken up positions in hills behind the agency. The Cheyennes had turned out to see the young warriors die bravely, the male spectators occupying the best vantage points, the women farther back.

Suddenly, across the valley about a rifle shot away, the spectators saw Head Chief and Young Mule ride from a patch of timber and head for the ridge above. Painted and befeathered—one boasted a magnificent war bonnet—they sang their war songs as they rode to the top of the hill. Reaching it they circled about, meanwhile opening fire on the cavalry and police below. As the Indians advanced and retreated, keeping up an intermittent fire, the cavalry on the road moved around the hill to outflank them. Faced with this threat, the two warriors charged down the hill, yelling and firing rapidly. A hail of fire knocked down one horse, but the young Indian continued on foot until he was hit. Taking cover, he disappeared from sight only to be tracked down later and found dead from gunshot wounds. The other Cheyenne did not slow his mad dash across the valley and up the opposite slope, careening through the police and cavalry lines before being felled. He wounded three horses in breaching the cavalry's line, the only damage inflicted on the soldiers and police. The entire action lasted about an hour, and the soldiers and police fired an estimated thousand rounds in the skirmish.

As the firing died away the bodies of Head Chief and Young Mule were recovered and brought to the agency. Echoing from the surrounding hills now was the wailing of the women as they viewed the battered young bodies. The troops, nervous and unable to comprehend what they had just participated in, were sure the women were inciting the Cheyenne men to avenge the youths. But a council called immediately by the agent brought only expressions of satisfaction from the Indians. Difficult to understand though it was for the whites, who regarded it as senseless bloodshed, the afternoon's proceedings could be reconciled with the Cheyenne concept of justice. The young warriors had acknowledged they had erred. They could not bring themselves to surrender to stand trial before strangers, perhaps to die disgracefully at the end of a rope. As had Satank, Head Chief and Young Mule would go as warriors should go, singing their war songs and counting coups. No wonder the Cheyenne women had wailed the loss of such fine youths. Although born too late to have ridden with Two Moons and White Bull against Custer, they had demonstrated that their generation still cherished the traditions of a warrior people.[20]

That the two young Cheyennes had chosen such a course of action testified to the ineffectiveness of Indian police and judges at Tongue River. A good police force would have prevented the crisis from developing. It would have kept the cattle off Indian land—Hugh Boyle was herding cattle when he was killed—and allayed the fears of the whites by keeping the Cheyenne messiah's followers under surveillance. Through their own Court of Indian Offenses the Cheyennes might have acquired some knowledge of American jurisprudence and, conceivably, some confidence in it.

Speculating about "what might have been" at Tongue River is one way of measuring the contribution Indian police

20. James A. Cooper to CIA, Sept. 14, 1890 (OIALR, 29222, 1890); Geo. W. Milburn and J. W. Strevell to Sec. of the Interior, Sept. 22, 1890 (Adjt. Gen. Doc. File, 15750, 1890); T. J. Porter to CIA, Sept. 23, 1890 (OIALR, 29887, 1890); AR of John Tully, 1891 (ser. 2934, pp. 286–87); Geo. W. H. Stouch to CIA, June 5, 1897 (ser. 3641, p. 83). Several years later another Cheyenne attempted, unsuccessfully, to emulate Head Chief and Young Mule. His agent reported the Indian was inspired to follow "in the footsteps of Head Chief and Young Mule, of whose heroic death stories are told around the fires, making every young man anxious for a similar death, so he, too, can become a brave and famous man." Geo. W. H. Stouch to CIA, June 5, 1897 (ser. 3641, p. 83).

and judges could make. Accepting the value judgment that change was not only inevitable but desirable, their service was obvious. Not only did they help convert reservations in a West notorious for lawlessness into "law and order havens," to use Clark Wissler's expression,[21] they were the vanguards of a more highly developed civilization. As Americans have had to make the transition from a rural–agrarian to an urban–industrial society, the Indians also have had to adjust to a new order. Granted this premise, it is patent that their own participation in the new law and order process would be beneficial. Casually conceived, only grudgingly accepted by the reformers and Congress, Indian police and judges were the happiest developments in what was too frequently a story of unrealistic policies and inefficient, if not corrupt, administration of a subject people.

21. Wissler, *Indian Cavalcade*, p. 136.

10. Epilogue

IT WAS the conjunction of administrative needs in the West, as exemplified in John Clum's experiences in Arizona, and the theorizing of Eastern administrators like Commissioner of Indian Affairs Edward P. Smith that launched the police experiment in 1878. Instituted at twenty-two agencies the first year, by the time the crisis precipitated by the messiah Wovoka hit the plains in 1890, there were forces at fifty-nine agencies—practically all. Although miserably paid and poorly equipped and uniformed, the police had already demonstrated their value to most agents, performing the multitude of services summarized by Secretary of the Interior Carl Schurz in 1880:

> Acting as guards at annuity payments and rendering assistance and preserving order during ration issues and protecting agency buildings and property; in returning truant pupils to school; in searching for and returning lost or stolen property, whether belonging to Indians or white men; in preventing depredations on timber and the introduction of whiskey on the reservation; in arresting or driving off whiskey-sellers, horse and cattle thieves; in making arrests for disorderly conduct, drunkenness, wife-beating, theft, and other offenses; in turning over offenders to the civil authorities; in serving as couriers and messengers; in keeping the agents informed as to births and deaths in the tribe; in notifying

him of the arrival on the reservation of strangers—
white or Indians; in accompanying and protecting sur-
veying parties, and, in general, such other duties as
in civilized communities are intrusted to an organized
police force.[1]

The Secretary's principal omission was perhaps deliberate:
the police at Apache reservations had also served as scouts
for army columns. He also failed to do justice to the policeman as the model reservation Progressive who abandoned
braids, cleaved to one wife, and sent his children to school.

The different roles played by George Sword on the Great
Sioux Reserve and Sam Sixkiller in the Cherokee Nation
illustrate extremes in the varieties of service police could
discharge. As captain of Indian police at Pine Ridge under
Dr. McGillycuddy, Sword's role was paramilitary in nature.
He headed a force of fifty men who were trained, not in
ordinary police duties, but as soldiers to fight as a unit under
military discipline. Herbert Welsh of the Indian Rights Association, for one, was convinced that the bloodshed at
Pine Ridge at the time of the Ghost Dance trouble need
not have occurred if McGillycuddy's successor had been as
successful as the doctor in substituting Indian police for
military control.

In contrast to George Sword, Sam Sixkiller's duties more
nearly corresponded to one of the fabled city marshals of
frontier days—a Wyatt Earp or a Wild Bill Hickok. Hostile
Indians in the plains sense were no problem at the Union
Agency of the Five Civilized Tribes, but bootleggers, cattle
thieves, train robbers, and cardsharps were. Sixkiller's experience differed in another important respect. Unlike Sword,
he became captain of police among a people who had a
well-developed judicial system. When he entered office in

1. AR of Schurz, 1880 (ser. 1959, p. 10).

1880 the Five Civilized Tribes had hierarchies of district, circuit, and supreme courts administering civil and criminal codes. Indeed, Sixkiller had served as High Sheriff of the Cherokee Nation. Admittedly the systems were more impressive on paper than in actual practice but, compared to the situation at Pine Ridge in the same period, they approximated what the reformers hoped to see evolve among the Sioux.

The absence, apart from the Five Civilized Tribes, of any provision for courts before which Indian police might bring their prisoners, impaired police effectiveness for several years. Lacking proper tribunals to pass judgment on those arrested by the police, agents acted as justices of the peace themselves or delegated the function to a subordinate. Federal courts were resorted to infrequently. Recourse to them was usually impractical because of jurisdictional problems, travel requirements, and language and cultural barriers. Proposals to remedy the situation were introduced into Congress, but were misunderstood because of their occasionally unrealistic nature, and suffered from the general stalemate caused by interdepartmental feuding. As Senator Alfred M. Scales explained his failure to introduce legislation to bring to the Indians the law about which he talked so much: "I believed that the first great step was to transfer the Indian Bureau to the War Department."[2] Not until 1883, five years after the police began to function, was the need for a local tribunal met by the creation of the first Court of Indian Offenses.

The hostility of Secretary of the Interior H. M. Teller to certain Indian religious and social practices and his concern with the persistence of these customs led him to urge Commissioner of Indian Affairs Hiram Price to find a solution. The result was the list of proscribed religious and social

2. *Congressional Record,* 10 (3) (1880), 2489.

practices and the Courts of Indian Offenses, which actually operated as police or justice of the peace courts. Agents were particularly happy to be relieved of the difficult and onerous task of passing judgment on Indian offenders and mediating family disputes. Being administrator of a reservation was sufficient trouble without having to play Solomon also.

The record of the court at the Yakima Agency for a period of about nine months in 1890 indicates some of the possibilities and problems of such a system. The Indians at the Yakima Agency represented a stage in civilization somewhere between that of Plains Indians and of the Five Civilized Tribes. Their justices, Stick Joe, Peal, and Louie Simpson all spoke some English. When on the bench they wore shirts and suits and conducted themselves with decorum. Of the thirty-one cases coming before them, thirteen involved property and nine stemmed from infractions of the moral code introduced by the white man. One adultery case was disposed of by a mandatory marriage ceremony performed promptly by the chief justice. In another, the couple was fined a total of $50 and charged $30 costs. Not all adultery convictions were so expensive. Johnnie Bullhead was found guilty of adultery with the wife of George Washington and it brought down on him a fine of only $1, with costs of $10, possibly indicating that the judges saw extenuating circumstances. Horses were involved in most of the property cases, and Chief Justice Stick Joe had to turn over a two-year-old horse and pay $5 costs when a judgment went against him in his own court.[3]

Two observations by the Yakima agent on the functioning of the court are significant: he had reversed the judgment in one case, and he noted that judges' salaries were coming from

3. AR of Warren L. Stabler, 1890 (ser. 2841, pp. 231–33).

fines and costs they levied on Indians before them. Employing policemen as judges was patently a bad practice, and the same might be said of drawing their salaries from fines they levied. But getting competent personnel to serve without compensation was impossible at most reservations.

Finances were always a problem for the Courts of Indian Offenses, but so was the power the agent wielded over them. The reformers looked upon the courts as only an expedient, to be replaced as soon as possible. The most frequent charge leveled against them was that they simply increased the agent's capacity for tyranny. Police were bad enough, but at least they always had been identified as an arm of the executive. The judiciary was supposed to be separate and equal; it violated all American constitutional principles to see judges the pawns of agents. In 1892 even Commissioner of Indian Affairs T. J. Morgan was brought to admit that the police and judges, "may be and sometimes are, merely instrumentalities in the hands of the agent for the enforcement of his power, which is now almost absolute."[4]

Even more damaging to the prestige of the Courts of Indian Offenses than the charge of agent domination were the challenges to their legality and jurisdiction. They administered a code proclaimed by the Secretary of the Interior, not legislated by Congress. Indeed, not until 1888, when a sum for their salaries was included in the appropriation bill, could it be said that they had any real legal existence. These developments did not solve the problem of jurisdiction which was aggravated yearly as the Dawes Act made available for purchase more and more reservation lands and the Indians and white populations mingled. And what of the allottee who claimed that as a landholder he was no longer subject to tribal government, or the white

4. AR of Morgan, 1892 (ser. 3088, p. 23).

man or mixed-blood caught in the toils of reservation law? The response of the Bureau of Indian Affairs was to continue the courts and police because they had become an administrative necessity, but to give way when challenged and to avoid expensive litigation and the possibility of unfavorable court decisions. The police and judges were operating in a constitutional twilight zone.

That they performed a valuable function was beyond doubt, and not only for the whites charged with administering the reservations but for the Indians as well. Indian courts and police served as a bridge between cultures. The pragmatic approach of the average agent meant that the relaxed and informal court procedures resembled the old tribal councils. The judges, who sought to compromise and conciliate rather than rule according to rigid points of law, were reminiscent of the tribal elders. Also, the police force occupied in some respects a place in Indian communities similar to that of the soldier society. Certainly his weapons and his prestige in the camps gave the policeman a status which was a link with his warrior past. As compared with the alternatives of military control, or the extension of state and federal legal codes over the tribesmen, the Indian police and courts afforded a reasonable solution to the problem of providing law and order. And, at the same time, they educated a minority people in a vital element of the dominant culture.

By 1900 the heyday of the police and judges was passing as they gradually were replaced by county and state officials. Here and there Indian police and judges would continue to function, but not on the scale of the 1890s or with the same objectives. In the first two decades of the twentieth century the reformers no longer talked with easy assurance of the civilizing properties of education, private property, Christianity, and law. Some progress had been made in destroying one way of life, but it was difficult to maintain that a satisfactory replacement had been found. But if Indian police and judges were no longer considered the hand-maidens of civilization, they were still indispensable in providing local law enforcement among some Indian populations. For another quarter century they would serve without fanfare, until another generation of reformers reawakened our conscience to the plight of the first Americans. Then the wisdom of the founders of the Indian police and Courts of Indian Offenses would be reaffirmed and these institutions refined and improved to meet new conditions and old objections. The success of Madeline Colliflower's appeal suggests that refinement and improvement are continuing, and that acculturation will gradually close the gulf separating the practices of Indian courts from the practices of other courts in our nation.

Bibliography

A. MANUSCRIPTS

1. National Archives
   Letters received by the Office of Indian Affairs (both manuscript and microfilm)
   Letter Books of the Office of Indian Affairs
   Secretary of the Interior Appointment File
   Adjutant General Document File
   Secretary of the Interior Hubert Work, "The Indian Courts," carbon copy in Tray 109, Records of the Board of Indian Commissioners

2. Oklahoma Historical Society
   Creek Foreign Relations File
   Kiowa Council File
   Kiowa Court File
   Kiowa Letter Book
   Kiowa Police File
   Oto Letter Books
   Ponca Letter Books
   Quanah Parker File
   Quapaw Police File
   Grant Foreman, "Indian-Pioneer History"

3. Library of Congress
   General August V. Kautz, Diary, 1877–1878 (microfilm copy)

4. Denver Federal Record Center
   Albiquiu Agency File
   Mescalero Apache Agency File
   Pueblo Agency File
   Southern Ute Agency File

5. Fort Worth Federal Record Center
   Union Agency File

B. GOVERNMENT DOCUMENTS

Congressional Record
Annual Reports of the Secretary of the Interior (including
   also reports of individual agents, Commissioners of
   Indian Affairs, Board of Indian Commissioners, Lake
   Mohonk Conferences, and sundry investigations)

C. NEWSPAPERS

1. Muskogee, *Indian Journal,* 1886–87
2. Prescott, *The Weekly Miner,* 1875–77
3. Tucson, *The Arizona Citizen,* 1875–77
4. Vinita, *Indian Chieftain,* 1886–87

D. THESES

Anderson, Harry H., "A History of the Cheyenne River
   Indian Agency and Its Military Post, Fort Bennett,
   1868–1891" (M.A. Thesis, University of South Da-
   kota, 1954).
Ballenger, Thomas Lee, "The Development of Law and
   Legal Institutions among the Cherokees" (Ph.D.
   Thesis, University of Oklahoma, 1938).
Buntin, Martha Leota, "History of the Kiowa, Comanche,
   and Wichita Indian Agency" (M.A. Thesis, University
   of Oklahoma, 1931).
Dutelle, Thomas E., "Development of Political Leadership
   and Institutions among the Klamath Indians" (M.A.
   Thesis, Columbia University, 1951).

Mardock, Robert Winston, "The Humanitarians and Post-Civil War Indian Policy" (Ph.D. Thesis, University of Colorado, 1958).

Swadesh, Frances L., "The Southern Utes and Their Neighbors 1877–1926" (M.A. Thesis, University of Colorado, 1962).

Waltman, Henry G., "The Interior Department, War Department and Indian Policy, 1865–1887" (Ph.D. Thesis, University of Nebraska, 1962).

E. OTHER PRINTED SOURCES

Bailey, L. R., *The Long Walk,* Los Angeles, Westernlore Press, 1964.

Benge, William B., "Law and Order on Indian Reservations," *Federal Bar Journal* (Summer 1960), pp. 223–29.

Berthrong, Donald J., *The Southern Cheyennes,* Norman, University of Oklahoma Press, 1963.

Boorstin, Daniel J., *The Americans: The Colonial Experience,* New York, Vintage Books, 1964.

Brown, Ray A., "The Indian Problem and the Law," *Yale Law Journal* (Jan. 1930), pp. 307–31.

Buntin, Martha, "Beginning of the Leasing of the Surplus Grazing Lands on the Kiowa–Comanche Reservation," *Chronicles of Oklahoma* (Sept. 1932), pp. 369–82.

Clum, John P., "The San Carlos Apache Police," *New Mexico Historical Review* (July 1929), pp. 203–19.

Clum, Woodworth, *Apache Agent: The Story of John P. Clum,* New York, Houghton Mifflin, 1936.

Cohen, Felix S., *Handbook of Federal Indian Law,* Washington, Government Printing Office, 1945.

Croy, Homer, *He Hanged Them High,* New York, Duell, Sloan and Pearce, 1952.

Davis, Laurence, "Court Reform in the Navajo Nation," *Journal of the American Judicature Society* (Aug. 1959), pp. 52–55.

———, "Criminal Jurisdiction over Indian Country in Arizona," *Arizona Law Review* (Spring 1959), pp. 62–101.

Ellin, Henry, "The Northern Arapaho of Wyoming," in Fred Eggan, ed., *Social Anthropology of North American Tribes,* Chicago, University of Chicago Press, 1955.

Ewers, John C., *The Blackfeet,* Norman, University of Oklahoma Press, 1958.

Finney, Frank F., Sr., "Progress in the Civilization of the Osage, and Their Government," *Chronicles of Oklahoma* (Spring 1962), pp. 9–11.

Foreman, Carolyn Thomas, "The Light-Horse in the Indian Territory," *Chronicles of Oklahoma* (Spring 1956), pp. 17–43.

Foreman, Grant, *The Five Civilized Tribes,* Norman, University of Oklahoma Press, 1934.

———, *Muskogee,* Norman, University of Oklahoma Press, 1943.

———, "The Tragedy of Going Snake Courthouse," *Daily Oklahoman* (Oct. 7, 1934), Section C, p. 14.

Fritz, Henry E., *The Movement for Indian Assimilation, 1860–1890,* Philadelphia, University of Pennsylvania Press, 1963.

Gibson, A. M., *The Kickapoos,* Norman, University of Oklahoma Press, 1963.

Goodale, Elaine, "Plain Words on the Indian Question," *New England Magazine* (April 1890), pp. 146–48.

Grinnell, George Bird, *The Fighting Cheyennes,* Norman, University of Oklahoma Press, 1956.

Hagan, William T., "Quanah Parker, Indian Judge," in K. Ross Toole et al., eds., *Probing the American West,* Santa Fe, Museum of New Mexico Press, 1962; also in *El Palacio* (Spring 1962), pp. 30–39.

Haines, Francis, *The Nez Percés,* Norman, University of Oklahoma Press, 1955.

Harrington, Fred Harvey, *Hanging Judge,* Caldwell, Idaho, Caxton Printers, 1951.

Harsha, William Justin, "Law for the Indians," *North American Review* (March 1882), pp. 272–92.

Hoebel, E. Adamson, *The Cheyennes,* New York, Holt, Rinehart, and Winston, 1960.

————, *The Law of Primitive Man,* Cambridge, Harvard University Press, 1954.

Humphrey, Norman D., "Police and Tribal Welfare in Plains Indian Cultures," *Journal of Criminal Law and Criminology* (July–Aug. 1942), pp. 147–61.

Hyde, George E., *Pawnee Indians,* Denver, University of Denver Press, 1951.

————, *Red Cloud's Folk,* Norman, University of Oklahoma Press, 1937.

————, *A Sioux Chronicle,* Norman, University of Oklahoma Press, 1956.

————, *Spotted Tail's Folk,* Norman, University of Oklahoma Press, 1961.

Keesing, Felix M., *The Menomini Indians of Wisconsin,* Philadelphia, American Philosophical Society, 1939.

Kneale, Albert H., *Indian Agent,* Caldwell, Idaho, Caxton Printers, 1950.

Lambertson, G. M., "Indian Citizenship," *American Law Review,* 20 (1886), 183–93.

"The Lawless Indian," *The Independent* (March 5, 1903), p. 576.

Leupp, Francis E., *The Indian and His Problem,* New York, Scribner's 1910.

Llewellyn, K. N., and E. Adamson Hoebel, *The Cheyenne Way,* Norman, University of Oklahoma Press, 1941.

Lowie, Robert H., "Property Rights and Coercive Powers of Plains Indian Military Societies," *Journal of Legal and Political Sociology* (April 1943), pp. 59–71.

McGillycuddy, Julia B., *McGillycuddy: Agent,* Stanford, Stanford University Press, 1941.

McLaughlin, James, *My Friend the Indian,* Boston, Houghton Mifflin, 1910.

Madsen, Brigham D., *The Bannock of Idaho,* Caldwell, Idaho, Caxton Printers, 1958.

Malone, Henry Thompson, *Cherokees of the Old South,* Athens, University of Georgia Press, 1956.

Mathews, John Joseph, *The Osages,* Norman, University of Oklahoma Press, 1961.

Mayhall, Mildred P., *The Kiowas,* Norman, University of Oklahoma Press, 1962.

Meriam, Lewis, *The Problem of Indian Administration,* Baltimore, Johns Hopkins Press, 1928.

Mooney, James, *The Ghost-Dance Religion and the Sioux Outbreak of 1890,* Washington, Bureau of American Ethnology, 1896.

Oliver, Symmes C., *Ecology and Cultural Continuity As Contributing Factors in the Social Organization of the Plains Indians,* Berkeley and Los Angeles, University of California Press, 1962.

"One Indian Lawman," in *Indians at Work* (October 1939), p. 11.

Price, Hiram, "The Government and the Indians," *Forum* (Feb. 1891), pp. 708–15.

Priest, Loring Benson, *Uncle Sam's Stepchildren,* New Brunswick, Rutgers University Press, 1942.

Provinse, John H., "The Underlying Sanctions of Plains Indian Culture," in Fred Eggan, ed., *Social Anthropology of North American Tribes,* Chicago, University of Chicago Press, 1955.

Prucha, Francis Paul, *American Indian Policy in the Formative Years,* Cambridge, Harvard University Press, 1962.

Richardson, Jane, *Law and Status Among the Kiowa Indians,* New York, Augustin, 1940.

Robinson, Doane, "The Education of Redcloud," *South Dakota Historical Collections, 12,* 176–78.

Schmeckebier, Laurence F., *The Office of Indian Affairs,* Baltimore, Johns Hopkins Press, 1927.

Shirley, Glenn, *Law West of Fort Smith,* New York, Collier Books, 1961.

Thayer, James Bradley, "A People Without Law," *Atlantic Monthly* (Nov. 1891), pp. 676–87.

Underhill, Ruth M., *The Navajos,* Norman, University of Oklahoma Press, 1956.

Vestal, Stanley, *New Sources of Indian History, 1850–1891,* Norman, University of Oklahoma Press, 1934.

Utley, Robert M., *The Last Days of the Sioux Nation,* New Haven and London, Yale University Press, 1963.

Walker, J. R., "The Sun Dance and Other Ceremonies of the Oglala Division of the Teton Dakota," in Clark Wissler, ed., *Sun Dance of the Plains Indians,* New York, American Museum of Natural History, 1921.

Wardell, Morris L., *A Political History of the Cherokee Nation, 1838–1907,* Norman, University of Oklahoma Press, 1938.

Welsh, Herbert, "The Meaning of the Dakota Outbreak," *Scribner's Magazine* (April 1891), pp. 439–52.

Whipple, Henry Benjamin, *Lights and Shadows of A Long Episcopate,* New York, Macmillan, 1902.

Wissler, Clark, *Indian Cavalcade,* New York, Sheridan House, 1938.

Index

Fig. 1. John P. Clum with Diablo and Eskiminzin, San Carlos, 1875

Fig. 2. John P. Clum and San Carlos Police, Tucson, May 1876

Fig. 3. Sam Sixkiller, Captain, Union Agency Police, c. 1885

Fig. 4. Ignacio, Captain, Southern Ute Agency Police, c. 1890

Fig. 5. Bert Arko, Captain, Kiowa Agency Police, c. 1895

Fig. 6. George Sword, Captain, Pine Ridge Agency Police, 1891

Fig. 7. Agent Lieutenant Maury Nichols and Kiowa Agency Police, 1891

Fig. 8. Sergeants Red Tomahawk and Eagle Man, Standing Rock Agency Police, c. 1890

Fig. 9. Standing Rock Agency Police, c. 1890

Fig. 10. Indian Police re-enacting shooting of Sitting Bull at his cabin, 1890

Fig. 11. Quanah Parker, c. 1895

Fig. 12. Quanah Parker with wives To-narcy and To-pay, c. 1895